Programming Puzzles
Python Edition

Contents

Getting Started

Welcome to the Programming Puzzles: Python Edition! Before you dive into the world of Python puzzles, let's cover a few essential points to ensure you have a smooth and enjoyable experience.

Introduction

The puzzles in this book have specifically been designed so that people of all levels can attempt them. You'll find some puzzles for people who are earlier along in their Python journey, and you'll find harder puzzles for people who are more experienced.

The book is broken up into two main sections, challenge puzzles and fun puzzles. The challenge puzzles section contains 50 (+ a few bonus) puzzles that start off at beginner level and get harder as you progress. This is the main section of the book and it's recommended you start on puzzle #1 and work your way through.

The fun puzzles section focuses more around being creative and making use of multiple libraries that Python offers. This section is recommended if you want a break from the challenge puzzles, although they still aren't easy!

Note: it's recommended you know at least the basics of Python before starting any puzzles from this book. Familiarity with fundamental concepts such as variables, conditionals, loops, and functions will greatly benefit you in solving the puzzles.

Environment Setup

It's important to get a working environment setup before you begin the puzzles - otherwise you won't be able to test your solutions! Luckily Python is pretty straightforward to get working.

Python Installation

Python installation will be different for everyone as it depends on your operating system, however as a general guide you can use the following steps:

1. Visit the official Python website at python.org

2. Navigate to the "Downloads" section.

3. Choose the appropriate installer for your operating system (Windows, macOS, or Linux) and **select a version of python that is 3.10 or greater**.

4. Download the installer and follow the instructions to complete the installation. If the installer asks if you'd like to install the pip package manager say yes.

After the installation is complete, you can open a command prompt or terminal and type *python --version* to verify that Python is installed correctly. It should display the version number you installed. If the version number isn't correct you can try *python3 --version* or *python3.10 --version*.

Code Editor

You will also need a code editor to edit and execute python code, there are many options out there but a few of the mainstream ones are:

- IDLE - comes bundled with Python.

- Visual Studio Code - code.visualstudio.com

- PyCharm - jetbrains.com/pycharm

In the scope of this book any of these editors will do the job, however as you continue your Python journey it's beneficial to move towards a more powerful IDE such as Visual Studio Code or PyCharm.

External Python Libraries

A small number of puzzles make use of external Python libraries. These can be installed using Python's package manager, pip.

You can check if you have pip by executing *python -m pip --version* in your command prompt / terminal. You should use the same python prefix as you did above, so if *python3 --version* worked for you above then you'd do *python3 -m pip --version* to check your pip version.

You can read more about pip at docs.python.org/3/installing/index.html

The external modules we use for the puzzles in this book can be installed by executing the following pip commands in your command prompt / terminal:

- *python -m pip install pygame*

- *python -m pip install PythonTurtle*

Git (optional)

This book comes with a provided git repository that contains starter code and solutions for each puzzle. This can be downloaded directly from github however the proper way is to clone it using a tool called git. If you're familiar with git, you can clone the repository as follows and then skip this section:

- *HTTPS: git clone https://github.com/MatWhiteside/python-puzzle-book.git*

- *SSH: git clone git@github.com:MatWhiteside/python-puzzle-book.git*

If you're unfamiliar with git you'll first need to install it on your computer, I won't cover it here as it can be different depending on your operating system but there are many guides that you'll be able to follow online.

If you can't get git to work it's not a big problem. Simply go to the github link in a browser and download the code as a zip file to your computer. You can then extract the file to a directory of your choosing and you're ready to go. Link: github.com/MatWhiteside/python-puzzle-book

A note on code snippets…

As you progress through this book, you may notice that certain code snippets, such as solutions, may appear with unconventional formatting. This formatting choice is intentional and allows the code to be properly printed within the pages of the book.

We strongly recommend that if you intend to execute the solutions or utilize the provided starter code, you consider cloning the GitHub repository associated with this book. By doing so, you will gain access to properly formatted and thoroughly tested code.

Big O Notation

There are a number of harder puzzles in this book that make reference to the time or space complexity of a problem. An example requirement could read like "ensure your solution has a maximum time complexity of O(n)" - but what does this mean?

The Big O notation is often used in identifying how complex a problem is and defines the worst case complexity for a particular piece of code. The Big O notation is written as: O(...).

Examples

O(1), also known as constant, indicates that the given code will always take the exact same amount of time regardless of the input. A constant function could look like:

```
def add_five(input_num):
    return input_num + 5
```

If the input_num = 0 or the input_num = 99999 the code still only has to execute one line to carry out the addition. Therefore, we have a constant time complexity.

O(n), also known as linear, indicates that the complexity increases with our input size. Our input is represented by the variable n. Let's take a look at what a linear function could look like:

```
def print_list(input_list):
    for item in input_list:
        print(item)
```

If the input_list has a length of 5, print(item) will execute 5 times. If the input_list has a length of 9999, print(item) will execute 9999 times. Therefore, we have a linear time complexity.

$O(n^2)$, also known as quadratic, indicates that the time complexity increases by our input squared as our input size increases. Let's take a look:

```python
def print_list_nested(input_list):
    for item in input_list:
        for inner_item in input_list:
            print(item, " + ", inner_item)
```

If the input_list has a length of 5, print(item, " + ", inner_item) will execute 25 times. If the input_list has a length of 1000, print(item, " + ", inner_item) will execute 1,000,000 times.

If you're confused, don't worry. There aren't mentions of the Big O notation until later in the book, and when you get there if you still need help you'll be able to find lots of resources online. Just google something along the lines of "Big O notation explained".

Final Points Before Starting…

Hopefully you're now fully set up and ready to start solving puzzles! There are just a few final points to note before you get going…

1. It doesn't matter if the solutions to your puzzles break for bad inputs. We're not writing production code here, if a puzzle states that the input will be a list of integers then assume that you will receive a list of integers. Do however think about edge cases e.g. what if the input list is empty? What if the input number is negative?

2. All of the challenge puzzles have starter code that's designed to get you going quickly. Most of them have just one function defined, however that doesn't mean you can't define more functions yourself. It's only a guide, you can even choose to not use the starter code at all; it's up to you!

3. A number of puzzles have caveats defined, these must be met to successfully complete the puzzle. If you're struggling, attempt the puzzle without the caveats met and then work out how you could improve your solution to meet them after.

4. Any code that is provided makes use of typing in the function definitions to make it obvious what the inputs and output of the function are meant to be. If you're not familiar with typing in python, don't worry it doesn't change anything from your side.

    In fact, if you really don't like the typing, feel free to delete it from the function definitions and carry on as usual!

    Example with typing:

    ```
    def filter_strings_containing_a(input_strs: list[str])
        -> list[str]:
    ```

    Example with typing removed:

    ```
    def filter_strings_containing_a(input_strs):
    ```

Challenge Puzzles

Welcome to the first section of the book, challenge puzzles. These puzzles are designed to start off easy and increase in difficulty as you work your way through.

Each puzzle will describe a task and ask you to implement a function to solve the task. To allow you to focus on the important part there is also starter code provided so you can get straight into coding!

Should you get stuck on any puzzle there is a hints section further down in the book, I highly recommend you use that section before looking at any solutions. The best way to progress is to struggle on a puzzle and then solve it by yourself.

Important: don't import any libraries unless specifically told in the puzzle!

Puzzle 1

Task

Define a function *filter_strings_containing_a* that takes one parameter:

Name	Type	Example Input
input_strs	list of str	["apple", "banana", "cherry", "date"]

When called, the function should return a new list containing only strings that contain the letter "a".

Starter Code

```
def filter_strings_containing_a(input_strs: list[str])
    -> list[str]:
    # Your implementation here

print(filter_strings_containing_a(
    ["apple", "banana", "cherry", "date"])
)
```

Examples

```
Input:  ["apple", "banana", "cherry", "date"]
Output: ["apple", "banana", "date"]

Input:  []
Output: []

Input:  ["bbbb", "cccc"]
Output: []
```

Puzzle 2

Task

Define a function *sum_if_less_than_fifty* that takes two parameters:

Name	Type	Example Input
num_one	int	20
num_two	int	25

When called, the function should return either:

- The sum of the two numbers if the sum is less than 50

- *None* if the sum of the two numbers is more than or equal to 50

Starter Code

```
def sum_if_less_than_fifty(num_one: int, num_two: int)
    -> int | None:
    # Your implementation here

print(sum_if_less_than_fifty(20, 20))
```

Examples

```
Inputs:
  - num_one = 20
  - num_two = 20
Output: 40
Inputs:
  - num_one = 20
  - num_two = 30
Output: None
Inputs:
  - num_one = 20
  - num_two = 100
Output: None
```

Puzzle 3

Task

Define a function *sum_even* that takes one parameter:

Name	Type	Example Input
input_nums	list of int	[1, 2, 3, 4, 5, 6, 7, 8, 9, 10]

When called, the function should return the sum of even integers in the list.

Starter Code

```
def sum_even(input_nums: list[int]) -> int:
    # Your implementation here

print(sum_even([1, 2, 3, 4, 5, 6, 7, 8, 9, 10]))
```

Examples

```
Input: [1, 2, 3, 4, 5, 6, 7, 8, 9, 10]
Output: 30

Input: [10, 20, 30, 40, 50]
Output: 150

Input: [9, 7, 5, 3, 1]
Output: 0
```

Puzzle 4

Task

Define a function *remove_vowels* that takes one parameter:

Name	Type	Example Input
input_str	str	"Hello, World!"

When called, the function should return a new string with all the vowels removed.

Starter Code

```python
def remove_vowels(input_str: str) -> str:
    # Your implementation here

print(remove_vowels("Hello, World!"))
```

Examples

```
Input: "Hello, World!"
Output: "Hll, Wrld!"

Input: "aeiouAEIOU"
Output: ""

Input: "zzxxxccvvvbbnnmmmLLKKJJHH"
Output: "zzxxxccvvvbbnnmmmLLKKJJHH"
```

Puzzle 5

Task

Define a function *get_longest_string* that takes one parameter:

Name	Type	Example Input
input_strs	list of str	["cat", "dog", "bird", "lizard"]

When called, the function should return the longest string in the list. If there are ties, return the string that appears first in the list.

Starter Code

```python
def get_longest_string(input_strs: list[str]) -> str:
    # Your implementation here

print(get_longest_string(["cat", "dog", "bird", "lizard"]))
```

Examples

```
Input: ["cat", "dog", "bird", "lizard"]
Output: "lizard"

Input: ["cat", "dog", "bird", "wolf"]
Output: "bird"

Input: ["a", "b", "c", "d"]
Output: "a"
```

Puzzle 6

Task

Define a function *filter_even_length_strings* that takes one parameter:

Name	Type	Example Input
input_strs	list of str	["cat", "dog", "fish", "elephant"]

When called, the function should return a new list with all the strings that have an even number of characters.

Starter Code

```
def filter_even_length_strings(input_strs: list[str])
    -> list[str]:
    # Your implementation here

print(filter_even_length_strings(
    ["cat", "dog", "fish", "elephant"]
))
```

Examples

```
Input: ["cat", "dog", "fish", "elephant"]
Output: ["fish", "elephant"]

Input: ["q", "w", "e", "r", "t", "y"]
Output: []

Input: ["qq", "ww", "ee", "rr", "tt", "yy"]
Output: ["qq", "ww", "ee", "rr", "tt", "yy"]
```

Puzzle 7

Task

Define a function *reverse_elements* that takes one parameter:

Name	Type	Example Input
input_nums	list of int	[1, 2, 3, 4, 5]

When called, the function should return a new list with all of the elements in the original list reversed.

Starter Code

```
def reverse_elements(input_nums: list[int]) -> list[int]:
    # Your implementation here

print(reverse_elements([1, 2, 3, 4, 5]))
```

Examples

```
Input: [1, 2, 3, 4, 5]
Output: [5, 4, 3, 2, 1]

Input: []
Output: []

Input: [20, 15, 25, 10, 30, 5, 0]
Output: [0, 5, 30, 10, 25, 15, 20]
```

Puzzle 8

Task

Define a function *filter_type_str* that takes one parameter:

Name	Type	Example Input
input_list	list of str or int	["hello", 1, 2, "www"]

When called, the function should return a new list containing only the strings from the original list.

Starter Code

```python
def filter_type_str(input_list: list[str | int]) -> list[str]:
    # Your implementation here

print(filter_type_str(["hello", 1, 2, "www"]))
```

Examples

```
Input: ["hello", 1, 2, "www"]
Output: ["hello", "www"]

Input: []
Output: []

Input: [1, 2, 3, 4, 5]
Output: []
```

Puzzle 9

Task

Define a function *string_to_morse_code* that takes one parameter:

Name	Type	Example Input
input_str	str	"HELLO, WORLD!"

When called, the function should return the more code equivalent of the input string. The function should meet the following requirements:

- A morse code "dot" should be represented by a full stop

- A more code "dash" should be represented by a hyphen

- A space should be used between each morse code letter e.g. ".-
  (space)-..."

- The function should be able to support the following characters in
  the input string:

  - Alphanumeric characters, uppercase and lowercase

  - Special characters: , . : ? ' - / ( ) " @ = + !

- Should a space be encountered in the input string, it should be
  represented as a forward slash in the output string

Starter Code

```python
def string_to_morse_code(input_str: str) -> str:
    morse_dict = {"a": ".-",      "b": "-...",   "c": "-.-.",
                  "d": "-..",     "e": ".",      "f": "..-.",
                  "g": "--.",     "h": "....",   "i": "..",
                  "j": ".---",    "k": "-.-",    "l": ".-..",
                  "m": "--",      "n": "-.",     "o": "---",
                  "p": ".--.",    "q": "--.-",   "r": ".-.",
                  "s": "...",     "t": "-",      "u": "..-",
                  "v": "...-",    "w": ".--",    "x": "-..-",
                  "y": "-.--",    "z": "--..",   "0": "-----",
                  "1": ".----",   "2": "..---",  "3": "...--",
                  "4": "....-",   "5": ".....",  "6": "-....",
                  "7": "--...",   "8": "---..",  "9": "----.",
                  ",": "--..--",".": ".-.-.-",":": "---...",
                  "?": "..--..","'": ".----.","-": "-....-",
                  "/": "-..-.",  "(": "-.--.",  ")": "-.--.-",
                  '"': ".-..-.","@": ".--.-.","=": "-...-",
                  "+": ".-.-.",  "!": "-.-.--"}

    # Your implementation here


print(string_to_morse_code("HELLO, WORLD!"))
```

Examples

```
Input: "HELLO, WORLD!"
Output: ".... . .-.. .-.. --- --..-- / .-- --- .-. .-.. -.. -.-
.--"


Input: "abcdefghijklmnopqrstuvwxyz,.:?'-/()\"@=+!"
Output: ".- -... -.-. -.. . ..-. --. .... .. .--- -.- .-.. -- -
. --- .--. --.- .-. ... - ..- ...- .-- -..- -.-- --.. --..-- .-
.-.- ---... ..--.. .----. -....- -..-. -.--. -.--.- .-..-. .--
.-. -...- .-.-. -.-.--"


Input: ""
Output: ""
```

Puzzle 10

Task

Define a function *get_second_Largest_number* that takes one parameter:

Name	Type	Example Input
input_nums	list of int	[1, 2, 3, 4, 5]

When called, the function should return the second largest number in the list. If there is no second largest number, the function should return *None*.

Starter Code

```
def get_second_largest_number(input_nums: list[int])
    -> int | None:
    # Your implementation here

print(get_second_largest_number([1, 2, 3, 4, 5]))
```

Examples

```
Input: [1, 2, 3, 4, 5]
Output: 4

Input: [3, 45, 345, 435, 345, 43, 56, 34, 234, 34]
Output: 345

Input: [1]
Output: None
```

Puzzle 11

Task

Define a function *format_number_with_commas* that takes one parameter:

Name	Type	Example Input
input_num	int	1000000

When called, the function should return a string representation of the number with commas as thousand separators.

Starter Code

```python
def format_number_with_commas(input_num: int) -> str:
    # Your implementation here

print(format_number_with_commas(1000000))
```

Examples

```
Input: 1000000
Output: "1,000,000"

Input: 12345
Output: "12,345"

Input: -99999999
Output: "-99,999,999"
```

Puzzle 12

Background

ASCII is a standard data-encoding format for electronic communication between computers. ASCII assigns standard numeric values to letters, numerals, punctuation marks, and other characters used in computers.

To convert a character to its ASCII code equivalent we can reference an ASCII table
- See: https://www.asciitable.com

The table has five headings: Dec, Hx, Oct, Html and Chr. To convert a character to its ASCII equivalent we find it in the Chr column and then take the corresponding number from the Dec column. For example, we can see "A" has the value of 65.

The conversion can also happen the other way, if we take the ASCII code 65 and look it up in the ASCII table we can see it matches up with the "A" character.

Task

Define a function *string_to_ascii* that takes one parameter:

Name	Type	Example Input
input_str	str	"Programming puzzles!"

When called, the function should return a list containing the ASCII numeric codes of each character of the string.

Starter Code

```
def string_to_ascii(input_str: str) -> list[int]:
    # Your implementation here

print(string_to_ascii("Programming puzzles!"))
```

Examples

```
Input: "Programming puzzles!"
Output: [80, 114, 111, 103, 114, 97, 109, 109, 105, 110, 103,
32, 112, 117, 122, 122, 108, 101, 115, 33]

Input: ""
Output: []

Input: "aA"
Output: [97, 65]
```

Puzzle 12.1 - Bonus

Task

Define a function *ascii_to_string* that takes one parameter:

Name	Type	Example Input
input_ascii_codes	list of int	[80, 114, 111, 103, 114, 97, 109, 109, 105, 110, 103, 32, 112, 117, 122, 122, 108, 101, 115, 33]

When called, the function should return a string consisting of the converted ASCII codes back to their char equivalents.

Starter Code

```
def ascii_to_string(input_ascii_codes: list[int]) -> str:
    # Your implementation here

print(ascii_to_string([80, 114, 111, 103, 114, 97, 109, 109,
105, 110, 103, 32, 112, 117, 122, 122, 108, 101, 115, 33]))
```

Examples

```
Input: [80, 114, 111, 103, 114, 97, 109, 109, 105, 110, 103,
32, 112, 117, 122, 122, 108, 101, 115, 33]
Output: "Programming puzzles!"

Input: []
Output: ""

Input: [97, 65]
Output: "aA"
```

Puzzle 13

Task

Define a function *filter_strings_with_vowels* that takes one parameter:

Name	Type	Example Input
input_strs	list of str	["apple", "banana", "zyxvb"]

When called, the function should return a new list with all the strings that have at least one vowel.

Starter Code

```
def filter_strings_with_vowels(input_strs: list[str])
    -> list[str]:
    # Your implementation here

print(filter_strings_with_vowels(["apple", "banana", "zyxvb"]))
```

Examples

```
Input: ["apple", "banana", "zyxvb"]
Output: ["apple", "banana"]

Input: []
Output: []

Input: ["q", "w", "e", "r", "t", "y"]
Output: ["e"]
```

Puzzle 14

Task

Define a function *reverse_first_five_positions* that takes one
parameter:

Name	Type	Example Input	Constraint
input_nums	list of int	[1, 2, 3, 4, 5, 6, 7, 8, 9, 10]	len(input_nums) == 10

When called, the function should return a new list with the first five
elements of the original list reversed. The solution should make use of
python slicing and should not use loops.

Starter Code

```
def reverse_first_five_positions(input_nums: list[int])
    -> list[int]:
    # Your implementation here

print(reverse_first_five_positions(
    [1, 2, 3, 4, 5, 6, 7, 8, 9, 10]
))
```

Examples

```
Input: [1, 2, 3, 4, 5, 6, 7, 8, 9, 10]
Output: [5, 4, 3, 2, 1, 6, 7, 8, 9, 10]

Input: [100, 90, 80, 70, 60, 50, 40, 30, 20, 10]
Output: [60, 70, 80, 90, 100, 50, 40, 30, 20, 10]

Input: [-1, -2, -3, -4, -5, -6, -7, -8, -9, -10]
Output: [-5, -4, -3, -2, -1, -6, -7, -8, -9, -10]
```

Puzzle 15

Task

Define a function *filter_palindromes* that takes one parameter:

Name	Type	Example Input
input_strs	list of str	["cat", "dog", "racecar", "deified", "giraffe"]

When called, the function should return a new list that contains only the strings that are palindromes.

Starter Code

```
def filter_palindromes(input_strs: list[str]) -> list[str]:
    # Your implementation here

print(filter_palindromes(
    ["cat", "dog", "racecar", "deified", "giraffe"]
))
```

Examples

```
Input: ["cat", "dog", "racecar", "deified", "giraffe"]
Output: ["racecar", "deified"]

Input: ["kayak", "deified", "rotator", "repaper", "deed", "a"]
Output: ["kayak", "deified", "rotator", "repaper", "deed", "a"]

Input: ["ab", "ba", "cd", "ef", "pt"]
Output: []
```

Puzzle 16

Task

Define a function *censor_python* that takes one parameter:

Name	Type	Example Input
input_strs	list of str	["python", "hello", "HELLO"]

When called, the function should return a new list of strings with the letters "P", "Y", "T", "H", "O", "N" replaced with "X", the solution should be case insensitive.

Starter Code

```python
def censor_python(input_strs: list[str]) -> list[str]:
    # Your implementation here

print(censor_python(["python", "hello", "HELLO"]))
```

Examples

```
Input: ["python", "hello", "HELLO"]
Output: ["XXXXXX", "XellX", "XELLX"]

Input: ["abcdefg"]
Output: ["abcdefg"]

Input: []
Output: []
```

Puzzle 17

Background

A string is happy if every three consecutive characters are distinct.

Example happy strings:
- "abcdefg"
- "qwerty"
- "abcabcabcabc"

Example unhappy strings:
- "aaaaaaaa"
- "cbc"
- "hello"

Task

Define a function *check_if_string_is_happy* that takes one parameter:

Name	Type	Example Input
input_str	str	"abcdefg"

When called, the function should return a bool indicating if the input string is happy or not.

Starter Code

```python
def check_if_string_is_happy(input_str: str) -> bool:
    # Your implementation here

print(check_if_string_is_happy("abcdefg"))
```

31

Examples

```
Input: "abcdefg"
Output: True

Input: "abcabcabcabc"
Output: True

Input: "hello"
Output: False
```

Puzzle 18

Task

Define a function *get_number_of_digits* that takes one parameter:

Name	Type	Example Input	Constraint
input_num	int	1234	input_num >= 0

When called, the function should return the number of digits in the *input_num*.

Caveats:

-   The function should be recursive

-   The function should not convert the integer to a string

Starter Code

```
def get_number_of_digits(input_num: int) -> int:
    # Your implementation here

print(get_number_of_digits(1234))
```

Examples

```
Input: 1234
Output: 4

Input: 0
Output: 1

Input: 123456789
Output: 9
```

Puzzle 19

Background

Tic-Tac-Toe (also known as naughts and crosses) is a two-player game played on a 3x3 grid. The objective of the game is to be the first player to get three of their symbols in a row, either horizontally, vertically, or diagonally. The game is played by alternating turns, with each player placing their symbol (usually an X or an O) on an empty space on the board until one player achieves a winning configuration or the board is filled without a winner, resulting in a tie.

A Tic-Tac-Toe board can be represented in python by a 2-dimensional list, with each of the inner lists representing a row. Let's look at an example:

```
input_board = [["X", "X", "X"],
               ["O", "X", "O"],
               ["X", "O", "O"]]

Represents the following game configuration:
X X X
O X O
X O O
```

Task

Define a function *get_tic_tac_toe_winner* that takes one parameter:

Name	Type	Example Input
input_board	list of list of str	[["X", "X", "X"], ["O", "X", "O"], ["X", "O", "O"]]

When called, the function should determine if X or O has won. If there is a draw the function should return *None*.

Starter Code

```python
def get_tic_tac_toe_winner(input_board: list[list[str]])
    -> str | None:
    # Your implementation here

print(get_tic_tac_toe_winner(
    [["X", "X", "X"], ["O", "X", "O"], ["X", "O", "O"]]
))
```

Examples

Input: [["X", "X", "X"], ["O", "X", "O"], ["X", "O", "O"]]
Output: "X"

Input: [["X", "O", "O"], ["O", "O", ""], ["X", "O", "O"]]
Output: "O"

Input: [["X", "O", "O"], ["O", "X", ""], ["X", "O", "O"]]
Output: None

Puzzle 20

Task

Define a function *print_triangle* that takes two parameters:

Name	Type	Example Input
number_of _levels	int	4
symbol	str	"*"

When called, the function should output a centred triangle shape made up of the desired symbol. The number of symbols in each row should increase by two with each level, starting with one symbol on the first level, then three on the second level and so on until the final level is reached. For example, for *number_of_levels* = 4 and *symbol* = "*" the following triangle should be produced:

```
   *
  ***
 *****
*******
```

Starter Code

```
def print_triangle(number_of_levels: int, symbol: str) -> None:
    # Your implementation here

print_triangle(4, "*")
```

Examples

```
Inputs:
 - number_of_levels = 3
 - symbol = "*"

Output:
  *
 ***
*****

Inputs:
 - number_of_levels = 1
 - symbol = "|"

Output:
|
```

Puzzle 21

Background

The Fibonacci sequence is a well-known mathematical series of numbers that has fascinated mathematicians and scientists for centuries. It is a sequence of numbers where each number in the sequence is the sum of the two preceding numbers. The sequence starts with 0, 1, and each subsequent number is the sum of the previous two numbers.

The sequence goes 0, 1, 1, 2, 3, 5, 8, 13, 21, 34, and so on.

Task

Define a function *fibonacci* that takes one parameter:

Name	Type	Example Input
sequence_number	int	4

When called, the function should return the corresponding fibonacci sequence number (starting from 0).

Caveats:

- The function should be recursive.

Starter Code

```python
def fibonacci(sequence_number: int) -> int:
    # Your implementation here

print(fibonacci(4))
```

Examples

```
Input: 4
Output: 3

Input: 0
Output: 0

Input: 6
Output: 8
```

Puzzle 22

Background

A harmonic sum is a mathematical concept that is used to calculate the sum of the reciprocals of a set of numbers. The reciprocal of a number is defined as 1 divided by the number. For example, the reciprocal of 2 is 0.5, because 1 divided by 2 is 0.5.

In the case of a harmonic sum, the set of numbers is usually represented by the natural numbers from 1 to n. The formula for the harmonic sum of n is: $Hn = 1/1 + 1/2 + 1/3 + ... + 1/n$.

Task

Define a function *harmonic_sum* that takes one parameter:

Name	Type	Example Input
n	int	5

When called, the function should return the harmonic sum of *n*.

Caveats:

- The function should be recursive.

Starter Code

```python
def harmonic_sum(n: int) -> float:
    # Your implementation here

print(harmonic_sum(5))
```

Examples

```
Input: 5
Output: 2.283

Input: 2
Output: 1.5

Input: 0
Output: 0
```

Puzzle 23

Background

The XOR (Exclusive Or) logic gate is a digital circuit that performs a logical operation on two inputs. The output of an XOR gate is true (1) if and only if one of the inputs is true and the other is false (0). In other words, the XOR gate compares the inputs, and if they are different, the output is true. If they are the same, the output is false.

This can be represented in a truth table, which is a table that shows the output of a logic gate based on all possible combinations of inputs. Here is an example of a truth table for the XOR gate:

Input A	Input B	Output
0	0	0
0	1	1
1	0	1
1	1	0

In this example, the left column represents input A, the middle column represents input B, and the right column represents the output. As you can see, when the inputs are different, the output is 1 and when the inputs are the same, the output is 0.

Task

Define a function *xor* that takes two parameters:

Name	Type	Example Input
input_a	str	"1101"
input_b	str	"0001"

When called, the function should return a string value that is the result of XOR'ing the two input strings together. If one string is longer than the other the excess characters should be ignored from the result.

Starter Code

```
def xor(input_a: str, input_b: str) -> str:
    # Your implementation here

print(xor("1101", "0001"))
```

Examples

```
Inputs:
  - input_a: "1111"
  - input_b: "1111"

Output: "0000"

Inputs:
  - input_a: "1111"
  - input_b: "0000"

Output: "1111"

Inputs:
  - input_a: "1101"
  - input_b: "00010"

Output: "1100"
```

Puzzle 24

Background

In Python, the zip function takes in one or more iterable objects (such as lists, tuples, or strings) and returns an iterator of tuples. Each tuple contains elements from each iterable object in the same position. The zip function stops when it reaches the end of the shortest iterable object.

Here is an example of how the zip function works:

```python
a = [1, 2, 3]
b = [4, 5, 6]

zipped = zip(a, b)
print(list(zipped)) # [(1, 4), (2, 5), (3, 6)]
```

Task

Define a function *my_zip* that takes two parameters:

Name	Type	Example Input
input_list_a	list of Any	[1, 2, 3, 4]
input_list_b	list of Any	[5, 6, 7, 8]

When called, the function should return the same result as python's built-in zip function.

Starter Code

```python
from typing import Any

def my_zip(input_list_a: list[Any], input_list_b: list[Any])
    -> list[tuple[Any, Any]]:
    # Your implementation here

print(my_zip([1, 2, 3, 4], [5, 6, 7, 8]))
```

Examples

```
Inputs:
 - input_list_a: [1, 2, 3, 4]
 - input_list_b: [5, 6, 7, 8]

Output: [(1, 5), (2, 6), (3, 7), (4, 8)]

Inputs:
 - input_list_a: []
 - input_list_b: []

Output: []

Inputs:
 - input_list_a: [1, 2, 3]
 - input_list_b: [5, 6, 7, 8]

Output: [(1, 5), (2, 6), (3, 7)]
```

Puzzle 25

Task

Define a function *is_valid_equation* that takes one parameter:

Name	Type	Example Input	Constraint
input_equation	str	"2 + 3 = 5"	The string should consist of an integer, followed by a plus or a minus sign, followed by another integer, an equals sign, and the answer. The equation should be separated by spaces.

When called, the function should return a boolean value indicating whether the equation is valid or not. The equation is classed as valid if:

- It's in the correct format as specified above

- Both sides of the equation evaluate to the same number

Starter Code

```
def is_valid_equation(input_equation: str) -> bool:
    # Your implementation here

print(is_valid_equation("2 + 3 = 5"))
```

Examples

```
Input: "2 + 3 = 5"
Output: True
Input: "-5 + -6 = -11"
Output: True
Input: "-2 + 3 = -5"
Output: False
```

Puzzle 26

Task

Define a function *rotate_list_left* that takes two parameters:

Name	Type	Example Input
input_list	list of Any	[1, 2, 3, 4, 5]
rotate_amount	int	2

When called, the function should return a new list with the elements of the original list rotated left by the specified number of positions.

Caveats:

- The solution should not make use of loops

- The function should still work if the rotation amount is greater than the length of the list, e.g. a rotation amount of 6 on a list of length 5 will produce the same result as if the rotation amount was 1.

Starter Code

```
from typing import Any

def rotate_list_left(input_list: list[Any], rotate_amount: int)
    -> list[Any]:
    # Your implementation here

print(rotate_list_left([1, 2, 3, 4, 5], 2))
```

Examples

```
Inputs:
 - input_list: [1, 2, 3, 4, 5]
 - rotate_amount: 2
Output: [3, 4, 5, 1, 2]

Inputs:
 - input_list: [1, 2, 3, 4, 5]
 - rotate_amount: 5
Output: [1, 2, 3, 4, 5]

Inputs:
 - input_list: [1, 2, 3, 4, 5]
 - rotate_amount: 7
Output: [3, 4, 5, 1, 2]
```

Puzzle 27

Background

An undirected graph is a mathematical representation of a set of objects in which some pairs of the objects are connected by links. The objects are represented by vertices (or nodes) and the links are represented by edges. In an undirected graph, the edges have no direction, meaning they can be traversed in both directions. It means if there is an edge between vertex A and B, then it is also true that there is an edge between vertex B and A.

A simple example of an undirected graph would be a group of cities and the roads connecting them. Each city would be represented by a vertex, and the roads connecting the cities would be represented by edges. It would not matter whether you are travelling from city A to city B or from city B to city A, the edge between them would still be the same.

It could look something like this:

```
A------B
|      |
|      |
C------D
```

Each letter represents a vertex (city) and the lines represent edges (roads). Here, A and B are connected by an edge and A and C are also connected by an edge.

Graphs are commonly represented in python using an adjacency matrix. The concept is simple, we have the list of nodes across the top and a list of nodes down the side. If two nodes are connected we place a "1" in the connection cell. If they're not connected we have a 0.

Example: Node A is connected to itself, Node B and Node C. Node B is only connected to node A. Node C is only connected to Node A.

	Node A	Node B	Node C
Node A	1	1	1
Node B	1	0	0
Node C	1	0	0

In python, this can be represented as a list of lists where each node is represented by an index. For example Nodes A, B, C would be represented by indexes 0, 1, 2 respectively:

```
graph = [
    [1, 1, 1],
    [1, 0, 0],
    [1, 0, 0]
]

graph[0][0] == 1 # Is Node A connected to itself?
graph[0][1] == 1 # Is Node A connected to Node B?
graph[2][1] == 1 # Is Node C connected to Node B?
```

Task

Define a function $find\_adjacent\_nodes$ that takes two parameters:

Name	Type	Example Input
adj_matrix	list of list of int	[[1, 1, 1], [1, 0, 0], [1, 0, 0]]
start_node	int	0

When called, the function should return a list of all nodes that are adjacent to $start\_node$.

Challenge: this challenge can be achieved with the function body being only one line of code, are you able to find the solution?

Starter Code

```
def find_adjacent_nodes(adj_matrix: list[list[int]],
start_node: int) -> list[int]:
    # Your implementation here

print(find_adjacent_nodes([[1, 1, 1], [1, 0, 0], [1, 0, 0]],
0))
```

Examples

```
Inputs:
 - adj_matrix: [[1, 1, 1], [1, 0, 0], [1, 0, 0]]
 - start_node: 0
Output: [0, 1, 2]

Inputs:
 - adj_matrix: [[1, 1, 1], [1, 0, 0], [1, 0, 0]]
 - start_node: 1
Output: [0]

Inputs:
 - adj_matrix: [[0, 1, 1, 0], [1, 0, 0, 1], [1, 0, 0, 1], [0,
1, 1, 0]]
 - start_node: 1
Output: [0, 3]
```

Puzzle 28

Background

In technical analysis, a peak refers to a high point or local maximum in the price of an asset. A valley, on the other hand, refers to a low point or local minimum in the price of an asset. When looking at a chart of the price of an asset, peaks and valleys can help traders identify potential turning points and potential changes in the overall trend of the asset.

For our sake, peaks and valleys are defined as the following:

- Peak:

    - A peak must have one or more numbers in ascending order leading up to it.

    - A peak must have one or more numbers in descending order after it.

    - A peak can not occur at the start or end of price action.

- Valley

    - A valley must have one or more numbers in descending order leading up to it.

    - A valley must have one or more numbers in ascending order after it.

    - A valley can not occur at the start or end of price action.

Task

Define a function *count_peaks_valleys* that takes one parameter:

Name	Type	Example Input
price_action	list of int	[1, 2, 3, 2, 1]

When called, the function should return a tuple representing how many peaks and valleys are in the given price action. The tuple should contain two integers, the first representing the number of peaks and the second representing the number of valleys.

Starter Code

```python
def count_peaks_valleys(price_action: list[int])
    -> tuple[int, int]:
    # Your implementation here

print(count_peaks_valleys([1, 2, 3, 2, 1]))
```

Examples

```
Input: [1, 2, 3, 2, 1]
Output: (1, 0)

Input: [1, 2, 3, 2, 1, 2]
Output: (1, 1)

Input: [7, 6, 5, 10, 11, 12, 10, 9, 10]
Output: (1, 2)
```

Puzzle 29

Background

Tap code is a simple method for transmitting messages through a series of taps or knocks. It was originally developed for prisoners of war to communicate with each other in secret, but it has also been used in other situations where communication is difficult, such as by hikers lost in the wilderness or by people trapped in a collapsed building. Tap code uses the following 5x5 grid to represent each letter:

	1	2	3	4	5
1	A	B	C / K	D	E
2	F	G	H	I	J
3	L	M	N	O	P
4	Q	R	S	T	U
5	V	W	X	Y	Z

Note: C and K are both represented by (1, 3) - when coding you can choose to either return C or K.

To transmit a message, the sender taps out the row and column of each letter in the message, with a pause between letters and a longer pause between words. The receiver then uses tap code to decode the message.

As an example, the word "water" would be represented by:
- 5, 2
- 1, 1
- 4, 4
- 1, 5
- 4, 2

Or when using in real life a series of taps: ••••• •• • • •••• •••• • •••••• ••••• ••

Task

Define a function *tap_code_to_english* that takes one parameter:

Name	Type	Example Input
input_code	str	".. ... ."

When called, the function should return the converted sentence. Items within the string should be represented as the following:

- Letters: 1-5 dots followed by a space, followed by 1-5 dots e.g. ". .." = "b"

- End of letter / start of new letter: two spaces e.g. ". .. . .." = "bb"

- End of word / start of new word: three spaces ".. ... ." = "hi hi"

Starter Code

```
tap_code_map = {
    "a": ".  .",
    "b": ".  ..",
    "c": ".  ...",
    "d": ".  ....",
    "e": ".  .....",
    "f": "..  .",
    "g": "..  ..",
    "h": "..  ...",
    "i": "..  ....",
    "j": "..  .....",
    "l": "...  .",
    "m": "...  ..",
    "n": "...  ...",
    "o": "...  ....",
    "p": "...  .....",
    "q": "....  .",
    "r": "....  ..",
    "s": "....  ...",
    "t": "....  ....",
```

```python
    "u": ".... ....",
    "v": "..... .",
    "w": "..... ..",
    "x": "..... ...",
    "y": "..... ....",
    "z": "..... ....."
}

def tap_code_to_english(input_code: str) -> str:
    # Your implementation here

print(tap_code_to_english(".. ...  .. ...    .. ...  .. ...."))
```

Examples

```
Input: ".. ...  .. ...    .. ...  .. ...."
Output: "hi hi"

Input: ". ...  ... ...    ... ...  ... ."
Output: "cool"

Input: ""
Output: ""
```

Puzzle 30

Task

Define a function *find_zero_sum_triplets* that takes one parameter:

Name	Type	Example Input
input_nums	list of int	[1, 2, 3, 4, 5, -9]

When called, the function should return all possible combinations of the indexes of three numbers that add up to 0. The function should return a list of tuples, each tuple containing the three indexes of the numbers that add up to 0, or an empty list if no such combination exists. The function should be able to deal with duplicate numbers in the input list.

Starter Code

```python
def find_zero_sum_triplets(input_nums: list[int])
    -> list[tuple[int, int, int]]:
    # Your implementation here

print(find_zero_sum_triplets([1, 2, 3, 4, 5, -9]))
```

Examples

```
Input: [1, 2, 3, 4, 5]
Output: []

Input: [1, 2, 3, 4, 5, -9]
Output: [(3, 4, 5)]

Input: [1, 2, 3, 4, 5, -9, -9]
Output: [(3, 4, 5), (3, 4, 6)]
```

Puzzle 31

Task

Define a function *param_count* that takes an arbitrary number of arguments.

When called, the function should return the number of arguments it was called with.

Starter Code

```python
from typing import Any

def param_count(*args: Any) -> int:
    # Your implementation here

print(param_count(1, 2, 3, 4, 5))
```

Examples

```
Inputs: 1, 2, 3, 4, 5
Output: 5

Inputs: "hello"
Output: 1

Inputs:
Output: 0
```

Puzzle 31.1 - Bonus

Task

Using the *my_zip* function from puzzle 24 as context, improve the function so that it can take an arbitrary number of arguments.

When called, the function should return the same result as python's built-in zip function. Your function can either return a list, or if you want to follow python's interpretation more closely it can return an iterator.

Starter Code

Return a list:

```python
from typing import Any

def my_zip(*input_lists: list[Any]) -> list[tuple[Any, ...]]:
    # Your implementation here

print(my_zip_one([1, 2, 3, 4], [5, 6, 7, 8], [9, 10, 11, 12]))
```

Return an iterator:

```python
from typing import Any
from collections.abc import Iterator

def my_zip(*input_lists: list[Any])
    -> Iterator[tuple[Any, ...]]:
    # Your implementation here

print(list(
    my_zip_two([1, 2, 3, 4], [5, 6, 7, 8], [9, 10, 11, 12])
))
```

Examples

```
Inputs: [1, 2, 3, 4], [5, 6, 7, 8], [9, 10, 11, 12]
Output: [(1, 5, 9), (2, 6, 10), (3, 7, 11), (4, 8, 12)]

Inputs: [1, 2, 3], [5, 6, 7, 8]
Output: [(1, 5), (2, 6), (3, 7)]

Input: [], []
Output: []
```

Puzzle 32

Task

Define a function *contains_python_chars* that takes one parameter:

Name	Type	Example Input
input_str	str	"Nohtyp"

When called, the function should return a boolean value indicating whether the string contains any combination of the word "python". The letters of "python" can be in any order e.g. "nohtyp" but must not be interrupted by any other characters. The function should be case-insensitive.

Starter Code

```
def contains_python_chars(input_str: str) -> bool:
    # Your implementation here

print(contains_python_chars("Nohtyp"))
```

Examples

```
Input: "pYThon"
Output: True

Input: "Nohtyp"
Output: True

Input: "pythZon"
Output: False
```

Puzzle 33

Background

A prime number is a positive integer that is divisible by only 1 and itself. It has no other positive divisors. Prime numbers are also often referred to as "primes" or "irreducible numbers". Some examples of prime numbers are 2, 3, 5, 7, 11, 13, 17, 19. They play an important role in number theory and have many applications in fields like cryptography, coding theory, and construction of pseudorandom number generators.

Task

Define a function *find_primes* that takes one parameter:

Name	Type	Example Input
input_nums	list of int	[1, 2, 3, 4, 5, 6, 7, 8, 9, 10]

When called, the function should return a new list containing only the prime numbers from *input_nums*.

Starter Code

```
def find_primes(input_nums: list[int]) -> list[int]:
    # Your implementation here

print(find_primes([1, 2, 3, 4, 5, 6, 7, 8, 9, 10]))
```

Examples

```
Input: [1, 2, 3, 4, 5, 6, 7, 8, 9, 10]
Output: [2, 3, 5, 7]

Input: [-1, -2, -3, -4, -5, -6, -7, -8, -9, -10]
Output: []

Input: [2, 3, 5, 7, 11, 13, 17]
Output: [2, 3, 5, 7, 11, 13, 17]
```

Puzzle 34

Background

ROT13 is a simple encryption technique that replaces each letter in a message with the letter 13 positions ahead of it in the alphabet. For example, "A" becomes "N", "B" becomes "O", and so on.

To calculate ROT13 for a given message, you simply need to shift each letter 13 positions ahead in the alphabet. If a letter is near the end of the alphabet and there are not enough letters left to shift it 13 positions ahead, you would wrap around to the beginning of the alphabet and continue counting.

Task

Define a function *rot13* that takes one parameter:

Name	Type	Example Input
input_str	str	"Hello world!"

When called, the function should return a new string which has been encrypted using ROT13. Numbers and symbols should not be rotated, they can be kept the same.

Starter Code

```
def rot13(input_str: str) -> str:
    # Your implementation here

print(rot13("Hello world!"))
```

Examples

```
Input:  "Hello world!"
Output: "Uryyb jbeyq!"

Input:  "Cool puzzles!"
Output: "Pbby chmmyrf!"

Input:  "12345!@£$%"
Output: "12345!@£$%"
```

Puzzle 35

Task

Define a function *get_parentheses_groups* that takes one parameter:

Name	Type	Example Input	Constraint
input_str	str	"(( )) (( )) ((( )))"	The parentheses in the string will always match up e.g. N opening parentheses should be followed by N closing parentheses.

When called, the function should return a list containing groups of fully matched parentheses without any spaces. Each parenthesis group should be one item in the list.

Starter Code

```
def get_parentheses_groups(input_str: str) -> list[str]:
    # Your implementation here

print(get_parentheses_groups("(( ))  (( ) ) (   (( )))"))
```

Examples

```
Input: "(( ))  (( ) ) (   (( )))"
Output: ["(())", "(())", "((()))"]

Input: "( ( ( ( ( ( ( ) ) ) ) ) ) )"
Output: ["(((((((())))))))"]

Input: ""
Output: []
```

Puzzle 36

Background

In mathematics, a matrix is a rectangular array of numbers, symbols, or expressions, arranged in rows and columns. Matrices are often labelled by capital letters, such as A, B, C, etc. Each element in a matrix is referred to by its row and column indices.

For example, consider the following matrix A:

```
[ 1  2  3 ]
[ 4  5  6 ]
[ 7  8  9 ]
```

This matrix has 3 rows and 3 columns, and its elements can be referred to as A_{ij}, where i is the row index and j is the column index. So, for example, $A\_12 = 2$ and $A\_31 = 7$.

Matrices can be used to represent large sets of data and operations can be performed on them such as matrix multiplication.

To perform matrix multiplication we need to ensure the number of columns of the left matrix equals the number of rows in the right matrix. Once that's confirmed, we can use the following steps:

1. Determine the size of the resulting matrix: the resulting matrix will have the same number of rows as the first matrix and the same number of columns as the second matrix.

2. Create a matrix of the correct size with all elements set to zero.

3. For each element in the resulting matrix, multiply the elements of the corresponding row in the first matrix and the corresponding column in the second matrix.

4. Sum up the products obtained in the previous step and assign the result to the corresponding element in the resulting matrix.

5. Repeat steps 3 to 4 for each element in the resulting matrix.

6. Return the resulting matrix.

Working example:

```
A = [[2, 3], [4, 5]]
B = [[10, 15], [5, 1]]
C = [[0, 0], [0, 0]]

C[0][0] = (A[0][0] * B[0][0]) + (A[0][1] * B[1][0])
C[0][1] = (A[0][0] * B[0][1]) + (A[0][1] * B[1][1])
C[1][0] = (A[1][0] * B[0][0]) + (A[1][1] * B[1][0])
C[1][1] = (A[1][0] * B[0][1]) + (A[1][1] * B[1][1])

Output: [[35, 33], [65, 65]]
```

Task

Define a function *matrix_multiply* that takes two parameters:

Name	Type	Example Input
left_matrix	list of list of int	[[2, 3], [4, 5]]
right_matrix	list of list of int	[[10, 15], [5, 1]]

When called, the function should return the result of the left and right matrix being multiplied together.

Starter Code

```
A = [[2, 3], [4, 5]]
B = [[10, 15], [5, 1]]

def matrix_multiply(
    left_matrix: list[list[int]], right_matrix: list[list[int]]
) -> list[list[int]]:

    # Your implementation here

print(matrix_multiply(A, B))
```

Examples

Inputs:
  - left_matrix: [[2, 3], [4, 5]]
  - right_matrix: [[10, 15], [5, 1]]

Output: [[35, 33], [65, 65]]

Inputs:
  - left_matrix: [[1, 2, 3, 4, 5, 6], [1, 2, 3, 4, 5, 6]]
  - right_matrix: [[1, 2], [3, 4], [5, 6], [7, 8], [9, 10], [11, 12]]

Output: [[161, 182], [161, 182]]

Inputs:
  - left_matrix: [[1, 2, 3, 4, 5, 6], [1, 2, 3, 4, 5, 6]]
  - right_matrix: [[1, 2, 3]]

Output: None

Puzzle 37

Background

The greatest common divisor of two or more integers is the largest positive integer that divides each of the integers without a remainder. For example, the GCD of 8 and 12 is 4, because 4 is the largest number that divides both 8 and 12 without leaving a remainder.

Task

Define a function *gcd* that takes two parameters:

Name	Type	Example Input
num_one	int	36
num_two	int	8

When called, the function should return the greatest common divisor of two integers.

Starter Code

```python
def gcd(num_one: int, num_two: int) -> int:
    # Your implementation here

print(gcd(36, 8))
```

Examples

```
Inputs:
  - num_one: 36
  - num_two: 8

Output: 4

Inputs:
  - num_one: 5
  - num_two: 25

Output: 5

Inputs:
  - num_one: 5
  - num_two: 26

Output: 1
```

Puzzle 38

Task

Define a function *find_pairs_summing_to_target* that takes two
parameters:

Name	Type	Example Input
input_num s	list of int	[1, 2, 3, 4, 5, 6, 7, 8, 9]
target	int	int

When called, the function should return a list of all pairs in *input_nums*
whose sum is equal to *target*.

Caveat:

- The resulting list should not contain duplicate pairs e.g. if
  input_nums=[5, 5, 5, 5] and *target=10* then the result should
  be [(5, 5)] instead of [(5, 5), (5, 5), (5, 5), (5, 5), (5, 5), (5, 5)].

Starter Code

```
def find_pairs_summing_to_target(
    input_nums: list[int], target: int
) -> list[tuple[int, int]]:

    # Your implementation here

print(find_pairs_summing_to_target(
    [1, 9, 2, 8, 3, 7, 4, 6, 5, 5], 10
))
```

Examples

```
Inputs:
 - input_nums: [5, 5, 5, 5]
 - target: 10
Output: [(5, 5)]

Inputs:
 - input_nums: [1, 2, 3, 4, 5, 6, 7, 8, 9]
 - target: 10
Output: [(1, 9), (2, 8), (3, 7), (4, 6)]

Inputs:
 - input_nums: [11, 12, 13, 14, 15]
 - target: 5
Output: []
```

Puzzle 38.1 - Bonus

Task

Improve the *find_pairs_summing_to_target* function from puzzle 38 so that it doesn't use nested loops. The inputs and output to the function will be the same. If your original solution didn't make use of nested loops then feel free to skip this bonus task.

Starter Code

```python
def find_pairs_summing_to_target_bonus(
    input_nums: list[int], target: int
) -> list[tuple[int, int]]:

    # Your implementation here

print(find_pairs_summing_to_target_bonus(
    [1, 9, 2, 8, 3, 7, 4, 6, 5, 5], 10
))
```

Examples

```
Inputs:
 - input_nums: [5, 5, 5, 5]
 - target: 10

Output: [(5, 5)]

Inputs:
 - input_nums: [1, 2, 3, 4, 5, 6, 7, 8, 9]
 - target: 10

Output: [(1, 9), (2, 8), (3, 7), (4, 6)]

Inputs:
 - input_nums: [11, 12, 13, 14, 15]
 - target: 5

Output: []
```

Puzzle 39

Background

The Tower of Hanoi is a mathematical puzzle that consists of three rods and a number of disks of different sizes which can slide onto any rod. The puzzle starts with the disks in a neat stack in ascending order of size on one rod, the smallest at the top, thus making a conical shape.

The objective of the puzzle is to move the entire stack to another rod, obeying the following rules:

1. Only one disk can be moved at a time.

2. Each move consists of taking the upper disk from one of the stacks and placing it on top of another stack or on an empty rod.

3. No disk may be placed on top of a smaller disk.

Task

Define a function *tower_of_hanoi* that takes four parameters:

Name	Type	Example Input	Description
num_disks	int	4	Number of disks starting on the source peg
source	str	"Source"	A string representing the source peg
aux	str	"Auxiliary"	A string representing the auxiliary peg
target	str	"Target"	A string representing the target peg

When called, the function should solve the Tower of Hanoi problem. The output should be printed to the console in the following format: "Move disk {n} from {peg} to {another_peg}" where n is the size of the disk. For example, the smallest disk will have size 1, the size up will be size 2, etc.

Starter Code

```python
def tower_of_hanoi(num_disks: int, source: str, aux: str,
target: str) -> None:
    # Your implementation here

tower_of_hanoi(4, "Source", "Auxiliary", "Target")
```

Examples

```
Inputs:
 - num_disks: 2
 - source: "Source"
 - aux: "Auxiliary"
 - target: "Target"
Output:
Move disk 1 from Source to Auxiliary
Move disk 2 from Source to Target
Move disk 1 from Auxiliary to Target

Inputs:
 - num_disks: 2
 - source: "Source"
 - aux: "Auxiliary"
 - target: "Target"
Output:
Move disk 1 from Source to Auxiliary
Move disk 2 from Source to Target
Move disk 1 from Auxiliary to Target
Move disk 3 from Source to Auxiliary
Move disk 1 from Target to Source
Move disk 2 from Target to Auxiliary
Move disk 1 from Source to Auxiliary
Move disk 4 from Source to Target
Move disk 1 from Auxiliary to Target
Move disk 2 from Auxiliary to Source
Move disk 1 from Target to Source
Move disk 3 from Auxiliary to Target
Move disk 1 from Source to Auxiliary
Move disk 2 from Source to Target
Move disk 1 from Auxiliary to Target
```

Puzzle 40

Background

Insertion sort is a simple sorting algorithm that builds the final sorted list one item at a time. It iterates through the input list, and for each element, it compares it to the elements that come before it and then inserts the element in the correct position. This process continues until all elements have been compared and placed in the correct position in the final sorted list.

It is called insertion sort because it can be thought of as inserting each element from the input list into its correct position in the final sorted list.

An example of insertion sort is sorting a deck of cards: starting with an empty left hand, we remove one card at a time from the deck with the right hand and place it in the correct position in the left hand.

Task

Define a function *insertion_sort* that takes one parameter:

Name	Type	Example Input
input_nums	list of int	[5, 10, 9, 11, 4]

The function should implement the insertion sort algorithm and return a sorted version of *input_nums* when called.

Starter Code

```
def insertion_sort(input_nums: list[int]) -> list[int]:
    # Your implementation here

print(insertion_sort([5, 10, 9, 11, 4]))
```

Examples

```
Input: [5, 10, 9, 11, 4]
Output: [4, 5, 9, 10, 11]

Input: [1, 2, 3, 4, 5]
Output: [1, 2, 3, 4, 5]

Input: [-1, -2, -3, -4, -5]
Output: [-5, -4, -3, -2, -1]
```

Puzzle 41

Background

Roman numerals are a numerical system that originated in ancient Rome and were widely used throughout the Roman Empire. They are a way of representing numbers using a combination of letters from the Latin alphabet. The system uses seven letters, each of which has a corresponding numerical value: I (1), V (5), X (10), L (50), C (100), D (500), and M (1000).

You can convert from integers to roman numerals using the following steps:

1. Create a lookup table for Roman numerals (see starter code).

2. Find the largest Roman numeral that is less than or equal to the integer, and subtract it from the integer.

3. Append the corresponding Roman numeral to the result string.

4. Subtract the corresponding integer value from the original integer.

5. Repeat steps 2, 3 and 4 with the remaining integer until the integer is 0.

6. Return the result string.

Task

Define a function *int_to_roman* that takes one parameter:

Name	Type	Example Input	Constraint
input_num	int	3000	The integer should be between 1 and 4999 inclusive.

When called, the function should return the input number converted to a roman numeral.

Remember to meet the following constraints of roman numerals:

1. You can only use the Roman numerals I, V, X, L, C, D and M, no other characters or notation is allowed.

2. You must follow the traditional rule of Roman numeral formation where smaller numerals are placed before larger numerals to indicate subtraction. For example, 4 is represented as IV, not IIII.

Starter Code

```
roman_map = {
    1000: "M", 900: "CM", 500: "D", 400: "CD", 100: "C",
    90: "XC", 50: "L", 40: "XL", 10: "X", 9: "IX", 5: "V",
    4: "IV",1: "I"
}


def int_to_roman(input_num: int) -> str:
    # Your implementation here

print(int_to_roman(4))
```

Examples

```
Input: 4
Output: "IV"

Input: 27
Output: "XXVII"

Input: 4999
Output: "MMMMCMXCIX"
```

Puzzle 41.1 - Bonus

Task

Define two extra functions: *roman_to_int* and *int_roman_converter*.

The *roman_to_int* function will carry out the reverse of the *int_to_roman* defined in puzzle 41. The function will take a string containing roman numerals and will return the corresponding integer.

Name	Type	Example Input	Constraint
input_str	str	"XXVII"	The representative integer should be between 1 and 4999 inclusive.

The *int_roman_converter* function will take either an integer or a string containing roman numerals. Depending on the input the function will either:

- Return the input integer converted to a roman numeral.

- Return the input string converted to an integer.

The function can determine whether it's been provided an integer or string by making use of pythons built in *isinstance* function.

Name	Type	Example Input	Constraint
to_convert	str or int	"XXVII"	The representative integer should be between 1 and 4999 inclusive.

Starter Code

```
# ...your solution to puzzle 41

def roman_to_int(input_str: str) -> int:
    # Your implementation here

def int_roman_converter(to_convert: str | int) -> int | str:
    # Your implementation here

for i in range(1, 5000):
    is_equal = int_roman_converter(int_roman_converter(i)) == i

    if not is_equal:
        print(f"{i} is incorrect!")
```

Examples

```
# roman_to_int examples
Input: "IV"
Output: 4

Input: "XXVII"
Output: 27

Input: "MMMMCMXCIX"
Output: 4999


# int_roman_converter examples
Input: "IV"
Output: 4

Input: 27
Output: "XXVII"

Input: "MMMMCMXCIX"
Output: 4999
```

Puzzle 42

Task

Define a function *bitwise_add* that takes two parameters:

Name	Type	Example Input
num_one	int	3
num_two	int	4

When called, the function should return the sum of the two input parameters.

Caveat:

- The function should not make use of any arithmetic operators.

Note: if you're not familiar with binary numbers you'll need to learn the basics before attempting this question. Google something along the lines of "introduction to binary numbers". You should also learn about logic gates.

Starter Code

```
def bitwise_add(num_one: int, num_two: int) -> int:
    # Your implementation here

print(bitwise_add(3, 4))
```

Examples

```
Inputs:
 - num_one: 3
 - num_two: 4
Output: 7

Inputs:
 - num_one: 255
 - num_two: 256
Output: 511

Inputs:
 - num_one: -1
 - num_two: -2
Output: -3
```

Puzzle 43

Background

Binary search is an efficient algorithm for finding an item from a sorted list of items. The basic idea behind the algorithm is to repeatedly divide the search interval in half until the value is found, or the search interval is empty.

To carry out a binary search the following steps can be executed:

1. Set the search interval equal to the whole list.

2. Calculate the middle element. If the length of the list is even, we take the lower middle element e.g. for [1, 2, 3, 4] we would say the middle element is 2.

3. The middle element of the search interval is compared to the value we are searching for, then:

    a. If the middle element is equal to the value we are searching for, the algorithm stops and returns the index of the element.

    b. If the middle element is greater than the value we are searching for, we know that the element we are searching for must be in the left half of the list. Therefore, the search interval is updated to be the left half of the current interval.

    c. If the middle element is less than the value we are searching for, we know that the element we are searching for must be in the right half of the list. Therefore, the search interval is updated to be the right half of the current interval.

4. The algorithm repeats step 3 with the updated search interval, until the value is found or the search interval is empty.

The functions steps can be represented using a simple walkthrough:

```
Sorted list = [2, 3, 4, 10, 40]
Value to find = 10

# Step 1
Search interval = sorted list
Middle element = 4

# Step 2
Is 10 equal to 4? No
Is 10 greater than 4? Yes
Is 10 less than 4? No

Search interval = [10, 40]
Middle element = 10

Is 10 equal to 10? Yes - value found
```

Task

Define a function *binary_search* that takes two parameters:

Name	Type	Example Input
sorted_list	list of int	[2, 3, 4, 10, 40]
value_to_find	int	10

When called, the function should perform a binary search on the *sorted_list* and return the index of *value_to_find* if present. If *value_to_find* isn't present in *sorted_list* the function should return -1.

Caveat:

- The function should have a time complexity of *O(log n)*

Starter Code

```python
def binary_search(sorted_list: list[int], value_to_find: int)
    -> int:
    # Your implementation here

searchable_list = [2, 3, 4, 10, 40]
print(binary_search(searchable_list, 10))
```

Examples

```
Inputs:
 - sorted_list: [2, 3, 4, 10, 40]
 - value_to_find: 10

Output: 3

Inputs:
 - sorted_list: [2, 3, 4, 10, 40]
 - value_to_find: 0

Output: -1

Inputs:
 - sorted_list: []
 - value_to_find: 0

Output: -1
```

Puzzle 44

Background

Quicksort is a divide-and-conquer algorithm that is used for sorting lists of items. It works by selecting a "pivot" element from the list and partitioning the other elements into two sub-lists according to whether they are less than or greater than the pivot. The sub-lists are then sorted recursively, which eventually results in the complete list being sorted.

The steps of the algorithm can be described as follows:

1. Choose a pivot element from the list. This element will be used to partition the list into two sub-lists.

2. Partition the list around the pivot element by moving all elements less than the pivot to the left of the pivot and all elements greater than the pivot to the right of the pivot.

3. Recursively sort the left sub-list.

4. Recursively sort the right sub-list.

5. Combine the sub-lists and the pivot to obtain the sorted list.

The choice of pivot element affects the performance of the algorithm. If a good pivot is chosen, the algorithm will be efficient, but if a poor pivot is chosen, the algorithm may become slow. A common strategy for choosing a pivot is to take the first, middle, or last element of the list.

Quicksort has an average time complexity of $O(n \ Log \ n)$, making it a very efficient sorting algorithm, especially for large lists. It is also an "in-place" sorting algorithm, which means that it does not require additional memory to sort the list as it sorts the list in place by exchanging elements within the list.

Task

Define a function *quicksort* that takes three parameters:

Name	Type	Example Input
input_list	list of int	[5, 7, 8, 1, 2, 4, 99, 77, 56, 43, 12, 98]
low	int	0
high	int	11

When called, the function should sort the *input_list* using the quicksort algorithm.

Starter Code

```
def quicksort(input_list: list[int], low: int, high: int)
    -> list[int]:
    # Your implementation here

unsorted_list = [5, 7, 8, 1, 2, 4, 99, 77, 56, 43, 12, 98]
print(quicksort(unsorted_list, 0, len(unsorted_list) - 1))
```

Examples

```
Inputs:
 - input_list: [5, 7, 8, 1, 2, 4, 99, 77, 56, 43, 12, 98]
 - low: 0
 - high: len(input_list) - 1

Output: [1, 2, 4, 5, 7, 8, 12, 43, 56, 77, 98, 99]

Inputs:
 - input_list: [10, 5, -10, -5, 0]
 - low: 0
 - high: len(input_list) - 1

Output: [-10, -5, 0, 5, 10]

Inputs:
 - input_list: []
 - low: 0
 - high: 0

Output: []
```

Puzzle 45

Background

Given a set of items, each with a weight and a value, and a knapsack with a limited capacity, determine the combination of items that maximises the total value while not exceeding the capacity of the knapsack.

The items are represented as a list of tuples where each tuple contains the weight and value of an item. The knapsack capacity is given as an input to the program.

Each item has a quantity of one.

Task

Define a function *solve_knapsack_problem* that takes two parameters:

Name	Type	Example Input	Description
items	list of tuples	[(5, 2), (1, 1000), (100, 1), (25, 25), (2, 1000)]	[(weight, value), ...]
knapsack_capacity	int	5	

When called, the function should return the maximum value possible without going over the weight restriction.

Starter Code

```python
def solve_knapsack_problem(
    items: list[tuple[int, int]], knapsack_capacity: int
) -> int:

    # Your implementation here

items = [(5, 2), (1, 1000), (100, 1), (25, 25), (2, 1000)]
max_weight = 5
print(solve_knapsack_problem(items, max_weight))
```

Examples

```
Inputs:
  - items: [(5, 2), (1, 1000), (100, 1), (25, 25), (2, 1000)]
  - knapsack_capacity: 5

Output: 2000

Inputs:
  - items: [(5, 2), (1, 1000), (100, 1), (25, 25), (2, 1000)]
  - knapsack_capacity: 0

Output: 0

Inputs:
  - items: []
  - knapsack_capacity: 5

Output: 0
```

Puzzle 45.1 - Bonus

Task

Improve your implementation of puzzle 45 to solve the knapsack problem in $O(nW)$ time complexity where n is the number of items and W is the capacity of the knapsack.

Starter Code

```
def solve_knapsack_problem(
    items: list[tuple[int, int]], knapsack_capacity: int
) -> int:

    # Your implementation here

items = [(5, 2), (1, 1000), (100, 1), (25, 25), (2, 1000)]
max_weight = 5
print(solve_knapsack_problem(items, max_weight))
```

Examples

```
Inputs:
 - items: [(5, 2), (1, 1000), (100, 1), (25, 25), (2, 1000)]
 - knapsack_capacity: 5

Output: 2000

Inputs:
 - items: [(5, 2), (1, 1000), (100, 1), (25, 25), (2, 1000)]
 - knapsack_capacity: 0

Output: 0

Inputs:
 - items: []
 - knapsack_capacity: 5

Output: 0
```

Puzzle 46

Task

Define a function *ip_range_to_list* that takes one parameter:

Name	Type	Example Input	Description
input_ip_range	str	"192.255.255.0-192.255.255.255"	The string should be formatted as the start IP followed by a dash followed by the end IP

When called, the function should return a list of all the unique IP addresses within the range, including the start and end IPs. Each IP address should be represented as a string in the format "x.x.x.x". The IP addresses should be in numerical order.

To make the solution as time efficient as possible the solution should make use of bitwise operations. You should make use of two libraries: struct and socket.

Starter Code

```python
import socket
import struct

def ip_range_to_list(input_ip_range: str) -> list[str]:
    # Your implementation here

print(ip_range_to_list("192.168.1.1-192.168.1.5"))
```

Examples

```
Input: "192.168.1.1-192.168.1.5"
Output: ["192.168.1.1",
         "192.168.1.2",
         "192.168.1.3",
         "192.168.1.4",
         "192.168.1.5"]

Input: "1.1.1.0-1.1.1.1"
Output: ["1.1.1.0", "1.1.1.1"]

Input: "192.255.255.0-192.255.255.0"
Output: ["192.255.255.0"]
```

Puzzle 47

Task

Define a function *solve_maze* that takes three parameters:

Name	Type	Example Input	Description
maze	list of list of int	[[0, 1, 1], [0, 0, 1], [1, 0, 1]]	A 2-dimensional list consisting of walls (1) and pathways (0). Each inner list represents a row of the maze with each n'th element representing the n'th column.
start_pos	tuple of (int, int)	(0, 0)	Starting position coordinates in the format (x, y).
end_pos	tuple of (int, int)	(1, 2)	Ending position coordinates in the format (x, y).

When called, the function should return a boolean indicating if the maze is solvable. The maze is only solvable if there is a pathway (all 0's) from the *start_pos* to the *end_pos*. The only valid moves in the maze are up, down, left and right - diagonal moves are not allowed.

Starter Code

```python
def solve_maze(
    maze: list[list[int]],
    start_pos: tuple[int, int],
    end_pos: tuple[int, int]
) -> bool:
    # Your implementation here

start = (0, 0)
end = (1, 2)

solvable_maze = [
    [0, 1, 1],
    [0, 0, 1],
    [1, 0, 1]
]

print(solve_maze(solvable_maze, start, end))
```

Examples

```python
# --- solvable maze example --- #
maze = [
    [1, 0, 1, 1, 1, 1, 1, 1, 1, 1],
    [1, 0, 0, 0, 0, 0, 0, 0, 0, 1],
    [1, 0, 1, 1, 1, 1, 1, 1, 0, 1],
    [1, 0, 1, 0, 0, 0, 0, 1, 0, 1],
    [1, 0, 1, 0, 1, 0, 0, 1, 0, 1],
    [1, 0, 1, 0, 1, 0, 0, 1, 0, 1],
    [1, 1, 0, 0, 1, 0, 1, 1, 0, 1],
    [1, 0, 0, 1, 0, 0, 0, 0, 0, 1],
    [1, 0, 1, 1, 1, 1, 1, 1, 1, 1],
    [1, 0, 1, 1, 1, 1, 1, 1, 1, 1]
]
start = (1, 0)
end = (1, 9)
def solve_maze(maze, start, end):
    ...

print(solve_maze(maze, start, end)) # Returns True
```

```python
# --- unsolvable maze example --- #

maze = [
    [1, 0, 1, 1, 1, 1, 1, 1, 1, 1],
    [1, 0, 0, 0, 0, 0, 0, 0, 0, 1],
    [1, 0, 1, 1, 1, 1, 1, 1, 0, 1],
    [1, 0, 1, 0, 0, 0, 0, 1, 0, 1],
    [1, 0, 1, 0, 1, 0, 0, 1, 0, 1],
    [1, 0, 1, 0, 1, 0, 0, 1, 0, 1],
    [1, 1, 0, 1, 1, 0, 1, 1, 0, 1],
    [1, 0, 0, 1, 0, 0, 0, 0, 0, 1],
    [1, 0, 1, 1, 1, 1, 1, 1, 1, 1],
    [1, 0, 1, 1, 1, 1, 1, 1, 1, 1]
]

start = (1, 0)
end = (1, 9)

def solve_maze(maze, start, end):
    ...

print(solve_maze(maze, start, end)) # Returns False
```

Puzzle 48

Background

In computer science a binary tree is a tree in which every node has zero, one or two children. If a node has children they are denoted by "left" or "right" children. A common action is to traverse the binary tree which is where we visit each node in a certain order and output the nodes values.

There are three main methods of traversal: pre-order, in-order and post-order. In this puzzle we're going to focus on in-order traversal, which works as follows:

1. Traverse the left subtree recursively by calling in-order traversal on the left child.

2. Visit the root node.

3. Traverse the right subtree recursively by calling in-order traversal on the right child.

Task

Define a function *traverse_inorder* that takes one parameter:

Name	Type	Example Input
root_node	TreeNode	TreeNode(4, two, six)

A TreeNode is a simple class we've created that has three properties:

Name	Type	Example
val	int	1
left_node	TreeNode	TreeNode(2, None, None)
right_node	TreeNode	TreeNode(3, None, None)

When called, the function should return an iterable containing the result of the in-order traversal.

Starter Code

```python
from __future__ import annotations
from typing import Iterator

class TreeNode:
    def __init__(
        self, val: int = 0,
        left: TreeNode | None = None,
        right: TreeNode | None = None,
    ) -> None:
        self.val = val
        self.left = left
        self.right = right

def traverse_inorder(root_node: TreeNode | None)
    -> Iterator[int]:
    # Your implementation here

one = TreeNode(1, None, None)
three = TreeNode(3, None, None)
two = TreeNode(2, one, three)
five= TreeNode(6, None, None)
four = TreeNode(4, two, five)

for node in traverse_inorder(four):
    print(node)
```

Examples

```
Input:
      4
    /   \
   2      6
  / \    / \
 1   3  5   7
Output: [1, 2, 3, 4, 5, 6, 7]

Input:
   2
  / \
 1   3
      \
       4
Output: [1, 2, 3, 4]
```

Puzzle 48.1 - Bonus

Background

The in-order traversal algorithm visits each node exactly once, so the time complexity of the algorithm is $O(n)$ and the space complexity is $O(h)$ where h is the height of the tree.

It is possible to perform an in-order traversal of a binary tree with constant space complexity $O(1)$ using the morris traversal algorithm. The algorithm works as follows:

1. Initialise the current node to the root of the tree.

2. If the current node has no left child, yield its value and move to its right child.

3. If the current node has a left child, find its in-order predecessor (i.e. the rightmost node in its left subtree):

   a. If the predecessor has no right child, set its right child to the current node and move to the left child of the current node.

   b. Else if the predecessor has a right child, reset its right child to None, yield the value of the current node, and move to the current node's right child.

Task

Write a python solution to implement the morris traversal algorithm. The inputs and outputs should be exactly the same as puzzle 48.

Starter Code

```python
from __future__ import annotations
from typing import Iterator

class TreeNode:
    def __init__(
        self,
        val: int = 0,
        left: TreeNode | None = None,
        right: TreeNode | None = None,
    ) -> None:
        self.val = val
        self.left = left
        self.right = right

def morris_traverse_inorder(root_node: TreeNode | None)
    -> Iterator[int]:
    # Your implementation here

one = TreeNode(1, None, None)
three = TreeNode(3, None, None)
two = TreeNode(2, one, three)
five = TreeNode(5, None, None)
seven = TreeNode(7, None, None)
six = TreeNode(6, five, seven)
four = TreeNode(4, two, six)

for node in morris_traverse_inorder(four):
    print(node)
```

Puzzle 49

Background

The climbing stairs problem is a common problem in computer science and mathematics. The problem involves finding the number of different ways someone can climb a set of stairs, where each step can be taken one at a time or two at a time.

The only input to the problem is the number of stairs in the staircase. For example, if the number of stairs in the staircase is 3, we have the following ways to climb the stairs:

-   1 step, 1 step, 1 step
-   1 step, 2 steps
-   2 steps, 1 step

Therefore, the answer to the problem would be 3.

Task

Define a function *solve_climbing_stairs_problem* that takes one parameter:

Name	Type	Example Input
total_stairs	int	4

When called, the function should return the number of possible combinations there are to climb the stairs.

Caveat:
-   The solution for this problem should make use of dynamic programming instead of simple recursion.

Starter Code

```python
def solve_climbing_stairs_problem(total_stairs: int) -> int:
    # Your implementation here

print(solve_climbing_stairs_problem(4))
```

Examples

```
Input: 4
Output: 5

Input: 10
Output: 89

Input: 0
Output: 0
```

Puzzle 49.1 - Bonus

Task

Your solution from puzzle 49 should output the total number of combinations possible, however it doesn't say what these combinations are.

Improve your solution so that the different combinations the staircase can be climbed in are returned.

Caveat:

- The solution for this problem should make use of dynamic programming instead of simple recursion.

Starter Code

```
def solve_climbing_stairs_problem_with_output(
    total_stairs: int
) -> list[list[int]]:
    # Your implementation here

print(solve_climbing_stairs_problem_with_output(4))
```

Examples

```
Input: 4
Output: [[1, 1, 1, 1], [2, 1, 1], [1, 2, 1], [1, 1, 2], [2, 2]]

Input: 10
Output: [[1, 1, 1, 1, 1, 1, 1, 1, 1, 1], [2, 1, 1, 1, 1, 1, 1,
1, 1], ...]

Input: 0
Output: []
```

Puzzle 49.2 - Bonus

Task

Modify your solution from puzzle 49 to allow for 1, 2 or 3 stairs to be climbed at once instead of just 1 or 2.

Caveat:

- The solution for this problem should make use of dynamic programming instead of simple recursion.

Starter Code

```
def solve_climbing_stairs_problem_with_three_steps_allowed(
    total_stairs: int
) -> int:
    # Your implementation here

print(
    solve_climbing_stairs_problem_with_three_steps_allowed(4)
)
```

Examples

```
Input: 4
Output: 7

Input: 10
Output: 274

Input: 0
Output: []
```

Puzzle 50

Background

Similar to puzzle 49, the coin change problem is a classic problem in computer science. The problem is defined as follows: given a set of coin denominations and a target amount, find the minimum number of coins needed to make the target amount.

Task

Define a function *solve_coin_change_problem* that takes two parameters:

Name	Type	Example Input
coin_values	list of int	[1, 6]
target_amount	int	6

When called, the function should return the minimum number of coins needed to make the target amount. The function should return -1 if it is not possible to reach the target.

We can assume there are an infinite number of each coin.

Caveat:

- Your solution should utilise dynamic programming to be as efficient as possible.

Starter Code

```
def solve_coin_change_problem(coin_values: list[int],
target_amount: int) -> int:
    # Your implementation here

print(solve_coin_change_problem([1, 6], 6))
```

Examples

Inputs:
 - coin_values: [1, 6]
 - target_amount: 6

Output: 1

Inputs:
 - coin_values: [1, 2]
 - target_amount: 6

Output: 3

Inputs:
 - coin_values: [2, 1]
 - target_amount: 13

Output: 7

Fun Puzzles

Welcome to the fun puzzles section! Puzzles in this section are designed to be a bit different, usually making use of external libraries that you may or may not have experience in. If you don't have experience using a specific library, don't skip the puzzle! It's a great chance to learn something new.

Reverse DNS lookup

Background

DNS (Domain Name System) is a system that translates human-readable domain names, such as example.com, into the IP addresses that computers use to identify each other on the internet. It works as a directory service, allowing users to access websites and other online resources by entering a domain name in their web browser. The domain name is then resolved into an IP address by DNS servers.

Task

Define a function *reverse_dns_lookup* that takes one parameter:

Name	Type	Example Input
ip_address	str	"8.8.8.8"

When called, the function should return the domain name that maps to that IP address using PTR DNS records. The function should return *None* if the IP address does not have a PTR record.

You should make use of the *gethostbyaddr* function found in the socket library.

Starter Code

```
import socket

def reverse_dns_lookup(ip_address: str) -> str:
    # Your implementation here

print(reverse_dns_lookup("8.8.8.8"))
```

Examples

Note: there's a small chance the outputs could change, if you get a slightly different response for these inputs the response is still likely to be correct.

```
Input: "8.8.8.8"
Output: "dns.google"

Input: "208.67.222.222"
Output: "dns.umbrella.com"

Input: "1.1.1.1"
Output: "one.one.one.one"
```

Russian Dolls

Background

Russian dolls, also known as Matryoshka dolls, are a set of wooden dolls of decreasing sizes that are placed one inside the other. The largest doll in the set typically opens up to reveal a smaller doll inside, which in turn contains an even smaller doll, and so on, until there are no dolls remaining.

Task

Define a function *unpack_dolls* that takes one parameter:

Name	Type	Example Input
doll	RussianDoll	RussianDoll(4, 3, "purple")

The parameter is of type *RussianDoll*, this is a simple class that contains three properties:

- Size - the size of the doll.

- Colour - the colour of the doll.

- Child doll - another *RussianDoll* object that this doll has inside of it, or *None*.

The *RussianDoll* class is given in the starter code below. When the *unpack_dolls* function is called it should have the same output as the example below.

Example

Given the following russian dolls:

Doll Size	Colour	Child Size
5	Grey	4
4	Purple	3
3	Green	2
2	Blue	1
1	Red	None

The program should have the following output to the console:

```
Unpacking a grey doll of size: 5 with 4 nested dolls inside.
Unpacking a purple doll of size: 4 with 3 nested dolls inside.
Unpacking a green doll of size: 3 with 2 nested dolls inside.
Unpacking a blue doll of size: 2 with 1 nested dolls inside.
Unpacking a red doll of size: 1 with 0 nested dolls inside.
Total number of dolls in the set: 5
```

Starter Code

```python
from __future__ import annotations

class RussianDoll:
    def __init__(
            self,
            size: int,
            colour: str,
            child_doll: RussianDoll | None = None
    ) -> None:

        self.size = size
        self.colour = colour
        self.child_doll = child_doll
```

```python
def unpack_dolls(doll: RussianDoll) -> int:
    # Your implementation here

doll_size_one = RussianDoll(1, "red", None)
doll_size_two = RussianDoll(2, "blue", doll_size_one)
doll_size_three = RussianDoll(3, "green", doll_size_two)
doll_size_four = RussianDoll(4, "purple", doll_size_three)
doll_size_five = RussianDoll(5, "grey", doll_size_four)
unpack_dolls(doll_size_five)
```

Fractal Tree

Background

A fractal tree is a tree-like structure that exhibits self-similar patterns at different scales, created by recursively applying a set of rules or algorithms to generate a branching pattern that looks similar to the structure of a real tree.

An example of a fractal tree can be seen to the below:

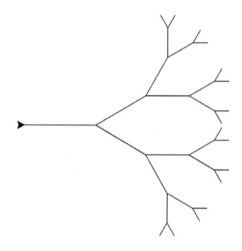

Task

Define a function *draw_tree* that takes one parameter:

Name	Type	Example Input
depth	int	5

When called, the function should display a fractal tree.

You should make use of the turtle graphics library that is built into python. If you're not familiar with the turtle graphics library, it provides a simple and user-friendly way to create graphics and visualisations using a virtual "turtle." The turtle is a cursor that can be controlled by a set of instructions to draw shapes and lines on a canvas.

Starter Code

```python
import turtle

def draw_tree(depth: int) -> None:
    # Your implementation here

draw_tree(5)
turtle.exitonclick()
```

Example

The tree depth of the tree above was depth 5. Your depth 5 tree should look exactly the same.

Ping pong

Task

Create a basic two player ping pong game using the pygame library. The game should have two paddles, one ball and implement a scoring system.

Note: challenges like this are most fun when letting the imagination run wild, so I've left the description purposely vague. There are no right or wrong answers here, as long as the final program represents some form of ping pong!

Bonus challenges:

- Allow the players to choose what colour they want the background, ball and paddles to be (*bonus-bonus: implement a visual colour picker*).

- Make the ball change colour every second.

- Allow an arbitrary number of balls to be in play at once.

Hint: the bonus challenges are easier to implement using object oriented programming (...think about having multiple balls at once).

Examples

As this is a creative puzzle each solution may well look completely different, and that's fine! Below are some examples of what a potential solution could look like.

Drawing Tool

Task

Create a basic drawing tool using the pygame library where a black canvas is displayed and the user can draw white coloured paint by clicking on the canvas.

Once the above application is complete we have a good base to add additional functionality to, here are some ideas as bonus challenges:

- Implement a sidebar that allows the user to:

    - Select a different drawing colour

    - Clear the canvas

    - Save their drawing to disk

    - Change the brush thickness
- Creating a line drawing tool so the user can choose between the "paint brush" and "line drawing tool"

…but don't stop there! These are just starter ideas and you can take your application in any direction you like!

Examples

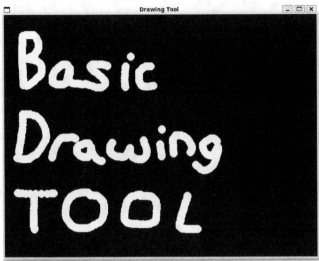

Challenge Puzzles: Hints

Puzzle 1

You will need to make use of a for loop to loop through each string in *input_strs*. Inside of the loop you will need to check if the current word contains the letter "a", this can be done using an if-statement.

To check if a string contains a letter you can use the "in" syntax e.g.

- *"a" in "banana" = True*

- *"a" in "pop" = False*

Puzzle 2

The first step to this puzzle is to sum together the two numbers.

The second step is to check if the resulting sum of the two numbers is less than 50. We can check this using an if statement, if the if statement is true (the sum is less than 50) then we return *None*. Else, we can return the result of the sum.

Puzzle 3

This puzzle can be broken down into a few steps...

The first step is to filter out odd integers, to do this we should make use of the modulo (%) operator. This operator works by giving us the remainder of a division e.g.

- *5 % 2 = 1*

- *4 % 2 = 0*

We can pair this operator with list comprehension to create a new list of only even integers. If you're not familiar with list comprehension it has the following syntax:

- *[<variable name> for <variable name> in <list> if <condition>]*

- The list comprehension: *[my_number for my_number in [1, 2, 3] if my_number % 3 == 0]* would result in *[3]* as *1 % 3 = 1* and *2 % 3 = 2* which makes our condition False.

We can then make use of Python's built in sum function. This function does what it says on the tin, sum's together all the elements of a list.

So if we create a new list with only even elements, then sum that list together and return the result... We're there!

Puzzle 4

This puzzle is a combination of the techniques learnt in puzzles 1 and 3.

We need to use a conditional list comprehension to loop through each character of our input string. The condition of the list comprehension should check if the current character is a vowel (hint: you can make use of the "in" syntax you used in puzzle 1). Once we have our resulting list, we can convert it to a string using the built in *join* function.

Puzzle 5

Let's start off by asking ourselves what's the longest string that we know of, before looking at the input strings? An empty string! The idea of this solution will be as follows:

- Define an empty string as our "longest string"

- Loop through each of the input strings and if the current string is longer than our "longest string" variable, then replace it.

- At the end, the string that's left in our "longest string" variable will be the longest!

You can use the built in *Len* function to get the length of a string.

Puzzle 6

I'm purposely going to leave the hints for this one short, the only hint I will give is to look at the techniques used in puzzles 3, 4 and 5.

Puzzle 7

Your solution here should make use of Python slicing. Python slicing is where we have square brackets after a list with the following syntax inside of the brackets: *start:stop:step*.

For example, if we take a list of [1,2,3,4,5,6] and a slice condition of [0:4:2] we would get a result of [1, 3]. This is because our slice condition is saying start at index 0 of the list (inclusive), stop at index 4 of the list (exclusive) with a step size of 2.

The number at index 0 of the list is 1, we then step forward 2 positions and take the number at index 2 of the list which is 3, then we step forward 2 more positions and that takes us past our stop condition so we're finished.

So what numbers would we need in our slicing condition to reverse the list? Hint: the step value can be negative!

Puzzle 8

For this puzzle you will need to make use of list comprehension and the built in *isinstance* function. This function works as follows:

- *isinstance(variable, type)* - if the type of the variable is equal to type then *True* is returned e.g.

    - *isinstance("a string", str) = True*

    - *isinstance("a string", int) = False*

Puzzle 9

Our solution should start off by initialising an empty list where we're going to store our result.

Then we need to loop through each character in the input string:

1. If the character is not a space, use the *morse_dict* to convert it to morse code and append it to our resulting list.

2. If the character is a space then we can append a forward slash to our resulting list.

Once we have our resulting list, we can join it together into a string using a similar technique to what we used in puzzle 4.

Puzzle 10

Let's break down our puzzle into steps:

1. Does the list contain at least two numbers? If not, return *None*.

2. Find the second largest number:

    a. Find and remove the maximum number from the list (hint: use the built in *max* function)

    b. We now know that in the remaining list the largest number is the second largest number of the original list. That means we can make use of the max function to find the largest number again, and return the result.

Puzzle 11

There are multiple ways to solve this solution however the most straightforward would be to make use of Python's f-strings. In Python, f-strings (formatted string literals) provide a concise and convenient way to embed expressions inside string literals, allowing you to create strings with dynamic content. They were introduced in Python 3.6 as a way to simplify string formatting compared to older methods like using the % operator or the .format() method.

Take a look at the Python f-string documentation and see what you can find!

Puzzle 12 & 12.1 - Bonus

In this solution we'll want to make use of Python's built in *ord* and *chr* functions:

- The *ord* function takes one character and returns the ASCII code equivalent of that value.

- The *chr* function takes an ASCII code and returns the character equivalent of that value.

Making use of these two functions along with techniques used in previous puzzles and you'll be on your way to solving this one!

Puzzle 13

This is the first solution where we might want to think about having a helper function. A helper function is simply another function that we can define and call inside of our *filter_strings_with_vowels* function.

Suggestion: define a second function called *has_vowel* that takes in an input string and returns *True* if the string contains a vowel, *False* otherwise.

We can then utilise a conditional list comprehension that makes use of our *has_vowel* function and filters the strings accordingly.

Puzzle 14

Use the slicing hints from Puzzle 7 to help you on this one!

Puzzle 15

Your solution here should make use of list comprehension and Python slicing. Maybe we could make use of the solution to puzzle 7 to help…

Puzzle 16

There are multiple stages to this solution that we need to think about:

1. Looping through each of the input strings

2. Looping through each of the characters of the input string and:

    a. Making the character case insensitive (hint: make use of Python's build in *upper* function)

    b. Checking if the character is equal to "P" or "Y" or "T" or "H" or "O" or "N"

    c. Replacing the character with an "X" if needed

3. Returning the list of strings with censored characters

A potential solution could make use of list comprehensions, the "*in*" keyword and the *join* function.

Puzzle 17

A potential solution to this problem could make use of three variables that move through the list and check if every three values are distinct. Imagine a solution that looks like the following:

```
input_str = "abcdefg"
a = input_str[0] = "a"
b = input_str[1] = "b"
c = input_str[2] = "c"

Are a and b and c different?
  - If yes, increment all of our indices and continue
  - If not, e.g. if a == b then the string would be unhappy

a = input_str[1] = "b"
b = input_str[2] = "c"
c = input_str[3] = "d"

Are a and b and c different?
  - If yes, increment all of our indices and continue
  - If not, e.g. if a == b then the string would be unhappy

... etc ...
```

It's not practical to hard code a solution like above, so how could we do it effectively in Python?

Puzzle 18

This is the first puzzle that is recursive, so if you're new to that concept, here is a quick rundown on recursion…

Recursion is a programming technique where a function calls itself in order to solve a problem. It's like a function looking into a mirror and asking itself for help to solve a smaller version of the same problem. This continues until the problem becomes simple enough to be directly solved.

Here's a basic example of recursion:

```
def countdown(n):
    if n <= 0:
        print("Go!")
    else:
        print(n)
        countdown(n - 1)

countdown(5)
```

This countdown function counts down from a given number n to 0. If n is less than or equal to 0, it prints "Go!". Otherwise, it prints the current value of n and then calls itself with n - 1 as the argument. This continues until n becomes 0 or negative, at which point the recursion stops.

Recursion usually has a base case where the function asks "under what condition should I stop calling myself?". In the example above this is the if n <= 0 part. If the base case isn't met, then we can carry on with recursion.

So let's think about puzzle 18…

- What do we want our recursion to do?

    - How about we (integer) divide *input_num* by 10 each time we recursively call the function?

        - 1234 // 10 = 123

        - 123 // 10 = 12

        - 12 // 10 = 1

        - 1 // 10 = 0

    - OK, so that works, but how are we going to count the number of digits?

        - Notice each time we carried out an integer division, one number was removed from *input_num*. So we could say each time the function is recursively called, add 1 to a count that will be returned when the base case is hit.

Taking that idea, I'll leave you with a second recursive example that gets the length of a string recursively…

```python
def get_length_of_str(input_str):
    # Base case
    if len(input_str) == 0:
        return 0

    # Recursive step that adds 1 to the count and removes a
    # character from the end of the input string
    return 1 + get_length_of_str(input_str[:-1])
```

Puzzle 19

This solution can be broken up into four parts:

1. Loop through all the rows and check if someone has won e.g. are all three values in the top row equal to "X"? If so, return "X".

2. Loop through all the columns and check if someone has won e.g. are all three values in the middle column equal to "O"? If so, return "O".

3. Check the diagonals and check if someone has won e.g. is the top left, middle and bottom right equal to "O"? If so, return "O".

4. If all of the conditions above are false, return None.

Puzzle 20

This puzzle needs some thinking about, but it can be done with one loop and a single print statement...

- The loop will represent each level of the triangle, starting at 1 and going all the way to *number_of_levels + 1*.

- The print statement should do the following:
    - Print the correct number of spaces
    - Print the correct number of symbols

How many spaces should be printed at each level?

- The number of spaces can be: *number_of_levels - current_level*. For example, if we have 5 levels and we're on level 1 then the number of spaces will be 4.

How many symbols should be printed at each level?

- The number of symbols can be: *current_level * 2 - 1*. For example, if we're on level two we'll want three symbols to show, so our formula would be 2 * 2 - 1 = 3.

Puzzle 21

After completing puzzle 18, we now know that recursion must have a base case and a recursive step. Let's think about these two conditions:

- Recursive step:

    - How is the fibonacci sequence calculated?

    - How can we make our recursive step calculate the sum of the previous two fibonacci numbers?

- Base case: if our recursive step is always calculating the sum of the previous two fibonacci numbers, at what point do we tell it to stop and return an actual number?

    - Hint: which numbers of the fibonacci sequence is it not possible to calculate the sum of the two previous numbers?

For extra clarity, let's look at what a recursion stack would look like:

```
fibonacci(4)

# Recursive step
= fibonacci(3) + fibonacci (2)

# Recursive steps of fibonacci(3) and fibonacci(2)
= fibonacci(2) + fibonacci(1) + fibonacci (1) + fibonacci (0)

# Recursive step of fibonacci(2)
# Base cases have been hit for fibonacci(1), fibonacci (1) and
fibonacci(0)
= fibonacci (1) + fibonacci (0) + 1 + 1 + 0

# Base cases have been hit for fibonacci(1) and fibonacci(0)
= 1 + 0 + 1 + 1 + 0

= 3
```

Puzzle 22

Hopefully you should be getting the hang of these recursive solutions! The key focus to solving this puzzle is focussing on the recursive step (the base case is similar, but not exactly the same to fibonacci).

So what does our recursive step need to do?

1. Calculate 1 divided by our current number (n).

2. Calculate the harmonic sum for all the numbers between n - 1 and 1 (hint: use recursion!).

If we sum together the result from steps one and two, then we have our recursive step!

Puzzle 23

As with every solution, the key to this puzzle is to break it down into parts:

1. Initialise a result string.

2. Loop through each of the input strings and carry out the XOR operation:

    a. Firstly, we'll need to work out the length of the shortest string. The reason we pick the shortest is because we're discarding any of the excess characters on the longest string.

    b. Next, we loop from 0 to the length of the shortest string and carry out the XOR operation on *input_a[current index]* and *input_b[current index]*.

    c. Depending on the result of the XOR we append a 0 or 1 to our result string.

3. Finally, return the result.

Puzzle 24

The solution to this puzzle should use very similar techniques to puzzle 23. Initialise a result variable, loop from 0 to the length of the shortest list and then append a pair tuple to the result.

Puzzle 25

The key piece of information when developing a solution to this puzzle is that each part of the equation is separated by spaces. This means that we can use Python's built in split function to break up the equation into parts.

Once we have the parts of the equation, we simply need to carry out the plus/minus calculation and then assert the results are equal.

Puzzle 26

We can't use loops for this puzzle so the solution should make use of list slicing. Your slicing should look something like this:

```
input_list[rotate_amount:] + input_list[:rotate_amount]
```

This will create the illusion of the list being rotated to the left. For example…

```
Inputs:
  - input_list: [1, 2, 3, 4, 5]
  - rotate_amount: 2

input_list[rotate_amount:] = [3, 4, 5]
input_list[:rotate_amount] = [1, 2]
input_list[rotate_amount:]
    + input_list[:rotate_amount] = [3, 4, 5, 1, 2]
```

The key part you need to work out is what should the value of *rotate_amount* be? Remember that the function should be able to deal with the rotate amount being larger than the length of the list. Hint: a potential solution can make use of the modulo operator (%).

Puzzle 27

This puzzle can be solved using one conditional list comprehension. The condition should make use of the following fact about conditionals in Python:

- "*if 1*" evaluates to True

- "*if 0*" evaluates to False

Your list comprehension should also make use of Python's built in *enumerate* function. If you're not familiar with this function it is used to add a counter to a list while looping through its elements. For example...

```python
my_list = ["a", "b", "c"]
for counter, value in enumerate(my_list):
    print(f"{counter}, {value}")
```

```
Output:
0, a
1, b
2, c
```

How could all of this be combined together to solve the solution?

Puzzle 28

Let's break this puzzle up into steps:

1. Initialise two variables to count the number of peaks and valleys detected.

2. Loop through each index of the list starting from 1 (not 0) and going all the way to $len(price\_action) - 1$. We'll call the index i for this hint.

3. Using $price\_action$, $i - 1$, i and $i + 1$ we can detect if there is a peak or a valley (this is for you to work out).

4. Once a peak or valley has been detected the appropriate count variable can be incremented.

5. Once the loop has finished, the count variables can be returned

Puzzle 29

The starter code has already given us the tap code dictionary to use in our solution, so let's think about how we can use it to convert one letter to tap code or vice versa. If we want to convert the letter "a" to tap code we can do *tap_code_map["a"]* which will return ". ." - however, this is the wrong way round. We want to convert ". ." to the letter "a".

To achieve this we need to invert our dictionary so that the keys are the values and the values are the keys. This is the first step to creating your solution. Hint: look up dictionary comprehension and think about how you could use it.

Step two is to have an if statement to check if the *input_code* is empty, if it is then we return an empty string.

Next, let's focus on how we'll process the actual code:

1. Break up the *input_code* into "tap code words", remember words are split by three spaces " "

2. For each tap code word:

   a. Split the word into individual letter tap codes, remember letters are split by two spaces " "

   b. For each letter tap code in the word:

      i. Use the inverted tap code dictionary to lookup the code and retrieve the letter value

   c. Join all of the letters of the word back together to create a string representing the word

3. Join all of the words of the sentence back together to create the human readable sentence

Puzzle 30

There is no need to overcomplicate this puzzle, all you need is a result list to add the combinations to and three for loops. I'll let you work out how they can be used to solve the puzzle!

Puzzle 31

Search google for "Python *args" - it'll give you everything you need! This puzzle is more of a warm up for 31.1.

Puzzle 31.1 - Bonus

Return a list...

Here is how a potential solution could work, try and implement each step as it's listed below:

1. Have a basic check for if the input list is empty, return an empty list.

2. Work out which is the shortest of the input lists - let's call this *shortest_length*.

3. Initialise a result object which will be a list of empty tuples where the number of tuples is equal to *shortest_length*.

4. Create a loop that loops from 0 to *shortest_length*, let's call the index *i*:

   a. Inside the loop, create another loop that loops through the *input_lists*:

      i. Append *input_list[i]* to the appropriate tuple in our result object.

5. Return the result object

Return an iterator…

I wouldn't recommend attempting this version before completing the "return a list" variation. If you've already completed that version here is some pseudocode that could help you to complete the iterator version:

```
def my_zip(*input_lists: list[Any])
    -> Iterator[tuple[Any, ...]]:

    sentinel = object()

    input_lists_iterators
        = a list of iterators for each input list in input_lists

    while input_lists_iterators is not empty:
        zipped_result = an empty List

        for each input_list_iterator in input_lists_iterators:

            get the next element from input_list_iterator,
            default to a sentinel value if there isn't a next
            element.

            # Check if the input list has been exhausted
            if the element is sentinel:
                exit loop

            add the element to zipped_result

        yield zipped_result as a Tuple
```

Puzzle 32

If you're stuck on this puzzle, think about how you could make use of sets. Remember sets are unordered, let's look at an example:

```
>>> set("hello") == set("oelhl")
True
```

Could you do something similar with detecting the letters of "python"?

Puzzle 33

A potential solution could make use of a helper function mixed with a conditional list comprehension. Similar to what we've done in the solution for puzzle 13.

The helper function only needs to work out if one number is prime and return *True* or *False* depending on if it is or not. To do that we can check two conditions:

1. Is the input number less than 2?

2. Can the number be divided by another number?

Puzzle 34

The first hint you can use to solve this issue is: could you make use of ASCII? Maybe some of the functions used in puzzle 12 and 12.1?

You can also use the following pseudocode to help:

```
def rot13(input_str: str) -> str:
    result = ""

    for each character char in input_str
        if char is an alphabetical character
            if char is an uppercase letter
                a_code = char_to_ascii("A")
            else
                a_code = char_to_ascii("a")

            char = ascii_to_char((
                char_to_ascii(char) - a_code + 13
            ) % 26 + a_code)

        append char to result

    return result
```

Puzzle 35

A potential solution to this puzzle would be to use a stack in the following way:

1. Initialise an empty stack.

2. Loop through each character of the input string.

3. If an open parenthesis is encountered then push it onto the stack.

4. If a close parenthesis is encountered then:

    a. If the stack is not empty:

        i. Pop an open parenthesis off of the stack.

        ii. If the stack is now empty you know you've detected a whole group. Add the group to the output string, replacing all the spaces as well.

5. Return the result string.

Puzzle 36

The first tip to solving this puzzle is to fully understand how to multiply two matrices, if there is any doubt then it'll be harder to solve the problem. There are many resources online explaining how to multiply two matrices together.

If you've fully understood how matrix multiplication works then let's look at some pseudocode for a potential solution, remember your solution doesn't have to look like this but this is one way it can be done.

```
def matrix_multiply(
    left_matrix: list[list[int]], right_matrix: list[list[int]]
) -> list[list[int]]:
    num_left_rows = get_number_of_rows(left_matrix)
    num_left_cols = get_number_of_columns(left_matrix)
    num_right_cols = get_number_of_columns(right_matrix)

    if num_left_rows != num_right_cols:
        return None

    result_matrix
        = create_empty_matrix(num_left_rows, num_right_cols)

    for i = 0 to num_left_rows - 1:
        for k = 0 to num_left_cols - 1:
            for j = 0 to num_right_cols - 1:
                result_matrix[i][j] +=
                    left_matrix[i][k] * right_matrix[k][j]

    return result_matrix
```

Puzzle 37

The main hint to this puzzle is that it can be done recursively. Think about the other recursive puzzles we've already got solutions for and how they could be adapted for this puzzle. What would the base case be? What would the recursive case be?

Extra hint: you can make use of the modulo (%) operator.

Puzzle 38

A potential solution could make use of nested loops, here is some pseudocode to help:

```
def find_pairs_summing_to_target(
    input_nums: list[int], target: int
) -> list[tuple[int, int]]:

    pairs = create_empty_list()

    for left_idx = 0 to length(input_nums) - 1:
        left_num = input_nums[left_idx]

        for right_idx = left_idx + 1 to length(input_nums) - 1:
            right_num = input_nums[right_idx]

            if left_num + right_num == target:
                pairs.append((left_num, right_num))

    return pairs
```

Puzzle 38.1

Here are some hints for solving the bonus puzzle without giving away too much:

- Your solution should use two sets:

    - One set will contain the resulting pairs.

    - One set will contain the numbers that we need to make a pair (called "seen" in our example).

- Your solution should use one for loop.

- Your solution should use one if-else statement.

Let's take a look at how some processing could look:

```
target = 10
input_nums = [1, 2, 9]
pairs = [] # Pairs of numbers that add up to target
seen = [] # Numbers that we need to make a pair

# Loop through each of the input_nums as input_num...

# Is target - input_num in seen?
10 - 1 in [] = False, so we add 1 to seen

target = 10
input_num = 2
pairs = []
seen = [1]

# Is target - input_num in seen?
10 - 2 in [1] = False so we add 2 to seen

target = 10
input_num = 9
pairs = []
seen = [1, 2]

# Is target - input_num in seen?
10 - 9 in [1, 2] = True so we add (9, 1) to our pairs
pairs = [(9, 1)]
```

Puzzle 39

The main hint to this puzzle is that it should be done recursively, however, this is harder than the other recursive tasks. You will need one base case but then two recursive steps with a print statement in between the two.

The good news is that is all you need. One base case followed by a recursive call, a print statement and then another recursive call. I'll let you work out the rest!

Puzzle 40

Insertion sort can be a tricky one to understand, but simple when you've mastered it! Here are some pointers on how to solve this puzzle:

- Begin by iterating through the input list of numbers.

- Conceptually divide the list into two parts: the sorted part and the unsorted part. Initially, the sorted part consists of only the first element, and the rest is unsorted.

- For each iteration, choose a value from the unsorted part of the list. This value will be inserted into its correct position within the sorted part.

- Compare the selected value with the elements in the sorted part of the list. Move the elements in the sorted part that are greater than the selected value to create space for the insertion.

- Once the correct position is found within the sorted part, insert the selected value at that position.

Once iteration is complete you will have a sorted list!

Puzzle 41

The key to this puzzle is to work out how to effectively use the
roman_map... Could you loop through it? Maybe make use of Python's built
in *sorted* function?

Puzzle 41.1

Let's start with the *roman_to_int* function. A potential solution could look like the following:

- Initialise a result variable and set its value to 0.

- Loop through each of the roman numerals in *input_str* and convert them to their respective numbers using the *roman_map*.

- Add the number to the result variable and continue until the *input_str* is exhausted.

However there's an issue, what about when subtraction is used? For example if *input_str* was equal to "IV" then the result should be 4, however using our above solution we would return 6. I'll leave you with one hint here:

- Roman numerals will always be in descending order unless subtraction is used. For example 16 = "XVI", X is greater than V which is greater than I. Could you use this information to detect subtraction, and deal with it accordingly?

- Example with subtraction 19 = "XIX", X is greater than I but I is less than X.

When it comes to writing the *int_roman_converter* function you can use the following pseudo code to help:

```
def int_roman_converter(to_convert: str | int) -> int | str:
    # roman numerals to int
    if to_convert is a string:
        return roman_to_int(to_convert)

    # int to roman numerals
    if to_convert is an int:
        return int_to_roman(to_convert)

    return None
```

Puzzle 42

To solve this puzzle you will need to make use of Python's bitwise operations, these work in the following ways:

```
# & (AND - left and right have to be 1)
1 & 1 = 1
1 & 0 = 0
0 & 1 = 0
0 & 0 = 0

# ^ (XOR - exclusive OR - left OR right has to be 1, not both)
1 ^ 1 = 0
1 ^ 0 = 1
0 ^ 1 = 1
0 ^ 0 = 0

# << (left shift - essentially doubles the number)
0b1 << 1 = 0b10
0b10 << 1 = 0b100
0b101 << 1 = 0b1010
```

Take some time to think about a solution, however if you're still stuck here is some pseudo code that should help:

```
def bitwise_add(num_one: int, num_two: int) -> int:
    while num_two is not 0:
        carry = some operation using AND...
        num_one = some operation using XOR...
        num_two = some operation using left shift...

    return num_one
```

Puzzle 43

The first step to solving this puzzle is to fully understand how the binary search works. There are plenty of resources online to help you learn, but make sure to not look at any Python solutions!

Once you've understood the fundamentals of how the algorithm works, you can use this pseudo code to get going:

```
def binary_search(sorted_list: list[int], value_to_find: int)
    -> int:

    low = 0
    high = length of the sorted_list - 1
    mid = 0

    while low is less than or equal to high:
        mid = average of high and low, rounded down

        if value_to_find is greater than the midpoint of the
        list, ignore left half by changing the low variable

        if value_to_find is smaller than the midpoint of the
        list, ignore right half by changing the high variable

        else, we have found value_to_find at sorted_list[mid]

    if we reach here, then the element was not present so
    return -1
```

Puzzle 44

Similarly to the binary search above make sure you fully understand the quicksort algorithm (it can take some time, it's a confusing one)! Once you've understood the algorithm you can make use of the pseudo code below to help with your implementation:

```
def quicksort(input_list: list[int], low: int, high: int)
    -> list[int]:

    if low < high:
        # Find the pivot index
        pivot_idx = partition(input_list, low, high)

        recursively sort the sublists by calling quicksort
        again twice...
          - once with low = low and high = pivot_idx - 1
          - once with low = pivot_idx + 1 and high = high

def partition(input_list: list[int], low: int, high: int)
    -> int:

    pivot = input_list[high]
    pivot_idx = low - 1

    for current_idx = low to high - 1:
        if the current element is less than or equal to the
        pivot:
          - move the pivot index to the right
          - swap(input_list[pivot_idx], input_list[current_idx])

    swap(input_list[pivot_idx + 1], input_list[high])

    return pivot_idx + 1
```

Puzzle 45

A potential solution to puzzle 45 is to use recursion - define a helper function that takes the following three parameters:

1. items - same as items in the solve_knapsack_problem function.

2. index - the index of the item (in items) we're considering adding to the knapsack.

3. remaining_capacity - the capacity we have left in the knapsack.

The function should have a base case and three recursive steps:

- Base case: have we considered all items, or is the capacity zero?

- Recursive steps:

  - If the current item's weight is more than the remaining capacity, we can't include it.

  - If the current item can be included:

    - Include it and recursively check the remaining capacity.

    - Don't include it and recursively check the remaining capacity.

This will check all possibilities for each item and return the correct answer.

Puzzle 45.1

Puzzle 45.1 asks us to improve our implementation of puzzle 45 to solve the knapsack problem in $O(nW)$ time complexity where n is the number of items and W is the capacity of the knapsack.

To achieve this we will need to use a concept called dynamic programming. Dynamic programming is simply an optimization of recursion where we store the results of subproblems. By storing the result it means we do not have to re-compute them when needed later.

Let's look at some pseudo code to base your solution off...

```
def solve_knapsack_problem_bonus(
    items: list[tuple[int, int]], knapsack_capacity: int
) -> int:

    # 2D matrix of zeros to store maximum values.
    # Rows = len(items) + 1. Columns = knapsack_capacity + 1.
    max_value_matrix = [[0, 0, ...], ...]

    for item_idx = 1 to len(items) + 1:
        for weight = 1 to knapsack_capacity + 1:

            # Check if the current item's weight exceeds the
            # remaining capacity
            if items[item_idx - 1][0] > weight:
                # Update the values in max_value_matrix
                max_value_matrix[item_idx][weight]
                    = max_value_matrix[item_idx - 1][weight]
            else:
                # Calculate the maximum value by considering
                # two options...

                # 1. Excluding the current item
                exclude_current = ...

                # 2. Including the current item
                include_current = ...
```

```
    # Choose the maximum of the two options
    max_value_matrix[item_idx][weight]
          = max(exclude_current, include_current)

# The final value in the matrix represents the maximum
# value achievable
return max_value_matrix[len(items)][knapsack_capacity]
```

Puzzle 46

The solution to puzzle 46 should follow the following logic:

- Split the input IP range into start and end IP addresses.

- Convert start and end IP addresses to their integer representations e.g. "1.1.1.1" = 16843009. This conversion is done in a couple of steps:

  - Convert each number of the IP address to binary data e.g. "1.1.1.1" = b'\x01\x01\x01\x01'.
    - Find the relevant function in the socket library.

  - Convert the binary data to an integer value e.g. b'\x01\x01\x01\x01' = 16843009.
    - Find the relevant function in the struct library.

- Loop from the converted start IP address to the converted end IP address and convert each integer back to an IP address, use the following steps:

  - Convert each integer to binary data e.g. 16843009 = b'\x01\x01\x01\x01'.
    - Find the relevant function in the struct library.

  - Convert the binary data to the IP address e.g. b'\x01\x01\x01\x01' = "1.1.1.1".
    - Find the relevant function in the socket library.

- Append the resulting IP addresses to a list and return.

Puzzle 47

If you're stuck on how to approach this puzzle take a look at how the breadth-first search algorithm works. You will want to implement it to solve the maze.

A possible solution could follow logic similar to the below:

```python
def solve_maze(
    maze: list[list[int]],
    start_pos: tuple[int, int],
    end_pos: tuple[int, int]
) -> bool:

    # Initialise variables
    num_rows, num_cols = len(maze), len(maze[0])
    queue = create_empty_queue()
    enqueue(queue, start_pos)
    mark_position_visited(maze, start_pos)

    # Start the exploration loop
    while queue is not empty:
        current_x, current_y = dequeue(queue)

        # Check if the current position is the end position
        if current_x == end_pos.x and current_y == end_pos.y:
            return True

        # Explore neighbouring positions
        for neighbor_x, neighbor_y in
            adjacent_positions(current_x, current_y):

            if is within maze bounds and is unvisited):
                enqueue(queue, (neighbor_x, neighbor_y))
                mark_position_visited(maze,
                                    neighbor_x,
                                    neighbor_y)

    # No path to the end position was found
    return False
```

Puzzle 48

This puzzle can be solved using one base case and two recursive steps. I'll let you work out what those should be!

Puzzle 48.1

The first step to writing the morris traversal algorithm is to fully understand how it works. As well as the resources on the puzzle, there are many resources online. Just be sure not to look at any Python solutions!

Once you've understood how the algorithm should work you can make use of the following pseudo code:

```
def morris_traverse_inorder(root_node: TreeNode | None)
    -> Iterator[int]:

    current_node = root_node

    while current_node is not None:

        if current_node has no left child:
            yield the value of current_node
            move to the right child of current_node
        else:
            find the predecessor_node by going right as far as
            possible from the left child of current_node

            if predecessor_node's right child is None:
                set predecessor_node's right child to be
                current_node

                move to the left child of current_node
            else:
                set predecessor_node's right child back to None
                yield the value of current_node
                move to the right child of current_node
```

Puzzle 49

The solution to this puzzle should make use of dynamic programming, so if you haven't completed previous puzzles e.g. 45.1 I would recommend doing that first.

To solve this puzzle we need to think about four main points:

1. Base cases: we know the answer if there are 0, 1 or 2 stairs so we can directly return a value.

2. Initialise the dynamic programming list with zeros and values we already know.

3. Fill the list by looping from 3 to *total_stairs + 1* and calculating the number of combinations for each number of stairs. This can be done using the previous values in the dynamic programming list.

4. Return the last position in the list which will represent the total number of combinations to climb the stairs.

Puzzle 49.1

The solution to this bonus puzzle will be similar to your solution for puzzle 49, however instead of keeping track of the number of combinations you need to keep track of the actual combinations.

The main changes will be:

- The base cases: instead of returning 2 if total_stairs = 2 we will return [[1, 1], [2]]

- The dynamic programming list: instead of storing 2 in position 2 we will store [[1, 1], [2]]

- Recursive steps: instead of just adding together the previous two values from the dynamic programming list, how can we keep track of the combinations of steps taken?

Puzzle 49.2

This solution should be a direct extension to your solution from puzzle 49. You will need an extra base case, two new values in the initial list and a slightly modified loop.

Puzzle 50

A potential solution to this puzzle could follow similar logic to the following:

- Check if the target amount is zero. If it is, you don't need any coins, so return 0 as the result.

- Check if the list of coin values is empty. If it is, you cannot make change with the given coins, so return -1 to indicate that it's not possible.

- Create a list called *min_num_coins* with a length of *target_amount + 1*, and initialise all its elements to infinity except for *min_num_coins[0]*, which is set to 0. This list will be used to keep track of the minimum number of coins needed to make change for each possible amount from 0 to the target amount.

- Now, loop through each target amount from 1 to the target amount + 1:

    - For each amount, loop through the available coin values:

        - Check if the current coin value can be used to make change for the current amount without going below zero (i.e., *current_target_amount - current_coin_value >= 0*).

        - If it's possible to use the current coin, update *min_num_coins[current_target_amount]* to be the minimum of its current value and the value obtained by adding 1 to *min_num_coins[current_target_amount - current_coin_value]*. This step effectively calculates the minimum number of coins needed to make change for the current amount.

- Finally, return the value stored in *min_num_coins[target_amount]*, which represents the minimum number of coins needed to make change for the original target amount using the provided coin values.

Challenge Puzzles: Solutions

Puzzle 1

```python
def filter_strings_containing_a(input_strs: list[str])
    -> list[str]:
    # Utilise list comprehension with an if condition to return
    # a new list consisting of strings that contain the letter
    # "a"
    return [input_str for input_str in input_strs if "a" in
input_str]
```

This solution makes use of list comprehension to create a new list of strings that have the letter "a" in them. The list comprehension iterates over the input list of strings and checks if each string contains the letter "a", if it does, it is included in the new list. The new list is then returned.

If you're not familiar with list comprehension, the above code is equivalent to the following:

```python
result = []

for input_str in input_strs:
    if "a" in input_str:
        result.append(input_str)

return result
```

Puzzle 2

```
def sum_if_less_than_fifty(num_one: int, num_two: int)
    -> int | None:

    # Calculate the sum of num_one and num_two, this avoids
    # calculating it twice on the return line
    summed_value = num_one + num_two

    # Return the summed value if it's less than 50, else return
    # None
    return summed_value if summed_value < 50 else None
```

This solution has two lines:

1. Add together the two input numbers

2. Return the sum of the two numbers if the value is less than 50

We make use of an if expression on the second line (not to be confused with an if statement!). The if expression is shorthand for the following code:

```
if summed_value < 50:
    return summed_value
else:
    return None
```

Puzzle 3

```
def sum_even(input_nums: list[int]) -> int:
    return sum(input_num for input_num in input_nums if
input_num % 2 == 0)
```

This solution can be broken up into three steps:

1. The sum function is called, with a generator expression as its argument. The generator expression iterates over each element *input_num* in the input list *input_nums* and filters out any odd numbers by checking if *input_num % 2 == 0* (i.e. if *input_num* is divisible by 2 with no remainder).

2. For each even number, the generator expression yields the value of *input_num*.

3. The sum function adds up all the values yielded by the generator expression, and returns the total sum of the even numbers in the input list.

Puzzle 4

```python
def remove_vowels(input_str: str) -> str:
    vowels = "aeiouAEIOU"
    return ""
        .join(char for char in input_str if char not in vowels)
```

This solution first defines a string containing all lowercase and uppercase vowels. We then use a generator expression to loop through each letter of the *input_str* and discard the letter if it's a vowel. The filtered letters returned from the generator expression are then joined back together and returned.

Puzzle 5

```python
def get_longest_string(input_strs: list[str]) -> str:
    longest_str = ""
    for input_str in input_strs:
        if len(input_str) > len(longest_str):
            longest_str = input_str
    return longest_str
```

This solution initialises an empty string called *Longest_str*. It then iterates over each string in the input list, and if the length of the string is longer than the length of *Longest_str*, the value of *Longest_str* is updated to the new string. Finally, the function returns the *Longest_str*.

Puzzle 6

```python
def filter_even_length_strings(input_strs: list[str])
    -> list[str]:
    return [input_str for input_str in input_strs
        if len(input_str) % 2 == 0]
```

This solution uses a conditional list comprehension to create a new list containing only the strings that have an even number of characters. The condition of `len(input_str) % 2 == 0` is saying "if the length of the string divided by 2 has a remainder of 0, then we include the string in our new list".

Puzzle 7

```python
def reverse_elements(input_nums: list[int]) -> list[int]:
    return input_nums[::-1]
```

This solution makes use of python slicing to reverse the list. Python slicing is where we have square brackets after a list with the following syntax inside of the brackets: *start:stop:step*.

For example, if we take a list of [1,2,3,4,5,6] and a slice condition of [0:4:2] we would get a result of [1, 3]. This is because our slice condition is saying start at index 0 of the list (inclusive), stop at index 4 of the list (exclusive) with a step size of 2.

The number at index 0 of the list is 1, we then step forward 2 positions and take the number at index 2 of the list which is 3, then we step forward 2 more positions and that takes us past our stop condition so we're finished.

In the case of this puzzle we have our slice condition as *[::-1]*, this is saying we have no start, no stop and a step size of -1 which means reverse. Having no start and no stop condition means we process the whole list and because our step size is -1 we do it in reverse.

Puzzle 8

```python
def filter_type_str(input_list: list[str | int]) -> list[str]:
    return [list_item for list_item in input_list
        if isinstance(list_item, str)]
```

This solution makes use of a conditional list comprehension similar to some of the above puzzles. The difference here is that we make use of pythons built in isinstance function. This function works by passing in a value and a type, it then returns *True* if the value is of the type specified and *False* if not.

For all the *list_item*'s where *True* was returned we add them to the new list and then return the result.

Puzzle 9

```python
def string_to_morse_code(input_str: str) -> str:
    morse_dict = {"a": ".-",      "b": "-...",   "c": "-.-.",
                  "d": "-..",     "e": ".",      "f": "..-.",
                  "g": "--.",     "h": "....",   "i": "..",
                  "j": ".---",    "k": "-.-",    "l": ".-..",
                  "m": "--",      "n": "-.",     "o": "---",
                  "p": ".--.",    "q": "--.-",   "r": ".-.",
                  "s": "...",     "t": "-",      "u": "..-",
                  "v": "...-",    "w": ".--",    "x": "-..-",
                  "y": "-.--",    "z": "--..",   "0": "-----",
                  "1": ".----",   "2": "..---",  "3": "...--",
                  "4": "....-",   "5": ".....",  "6": "-....",
                  "7": "--...",   "8": "---..",  "9": "----.",
                  ",": "--..--",  ".": ".-.-.-", ":": "---...",
                  "?": "..--..",  "'": ".----.", "-": "-....-",
                  "/": "-..-.",   "(": "-.--.",  ")": "-.--.-",
                  '"': ".-..-.",  "@": ".--.-.", "=": "-...-",
                  "+": ".-.-.",   "!": "-.-.--"}
    morse = []
    for char in input_str:
        if char != " ":
            char = char.lower()
            morse.append(morse_dict[char])
        else:
            morse.append("/")
    return " ".join(morse)
```

This solution iterates through each character in *input_str*, converts it to lowercase, and uses the *morse_dict* to look up the morse code equivalent. If the character encountered is a space it is represented by a forward slash. The morse code equivalent is appended to the *morse* list.

After iterating through all the characters the morse list is returned with spaces between each code.

Puzzle 10

```python
def get_second_largest_number(input_nums: list[int])
    -> int | None:

    if len(input_nums) < 2:
        return None

    max_number = max(input_nums)
    input_nums.remove(max_number)
    second_max = max(input_nums)

    return second_max
```

This solution first checks if the length of *input_nums* is less than two, if there are less than two numbers in *input_nums* we return *None* as it's not possible to get a second largest number.

The second largest number is then calculated by finding and removing the maximum number from the list, then finding the maximum number again and returning it.

Puzzle 11

```
def format_number_with_commas(input_num: int) -> str:
    return f"{input_num:,}"
```

This solution uses an f-string to format the number correctly, it works in the following way:

- The f before the string indicates that this is a formatted string literal

- Inside the curly braces, the colon specifies that we want to apply a formatting option

- The comma after the colon specifies that we want to use a comma separator for every thousand in the number

Puzzle 12

```python
def string_to_ascii(input_str: str) -> list[int]:
    return [ord(char) for char in input_str]
```

This solution makes use of pythons built in *ord* function to convert each letter of the string to its ASCII equivalent. List comprehension is used so that the results of the conversion are added to a list and returned.

Puzzle 12.1 - Bonus Solution

```python
def ascii_to_string(input_ascii_codes: list[int]) -> str:
    return "".join([chr(input_ascii_code)
        for input_ascii_code in input_ascii_codes])
```

This solution is very similar to the above, however makes use of the built in *chr* function to convert from ASCII numeric values to their representative characters. The resulting list is then joined to create the returned string.

Puzzle 13

```python
def has_vowel(input_str: str) -> bool:
    vowels = "aeiouAEIOU"
    for char in input_str:
        if char in vowels:
            return True
    return False


def filter_strings_with_vowels(input_strs: list[str])
    -> list[str]:

    return [input_str for input_str in input_strs
        if has_vowel(input_str)]
```

This solution defines an additional function *has_vowel* that takes a string and returns *True* if it contains a vowel and *False* otherwise.

The *filter_strings_with_vowels* function uses list comprehension to iterate over *input_strs* and keep only the strings for which *has_vowel* returns *True*.

Puzzle 14

```python
def reverse_first_five_positions(input_nums: list[int])
    -> list[int]:

    return input_nums[:5][::-1] + input_nums[5:]
```

This solution makes use of slicing and list addition to rotate the first five positions. The easiest way to follow how it works is by taking an example:

```python
# Initial input
input_nums = [1, 2, 3, 4, 5, 6, 7, 8, 9, 10]

# Slice the first five numbers, then reverse the result
input_nums[:5][::-1] = [5, 4, 3, 2, 1]

# Slice the rest of the numbers after the first five
input_nums[5:] = [6, 7, 8, 9, 10]

# Add together the above two results
input_nums[:5][::-1] + input_nums[5:]
    = [5, 4, 3, 2, 1, 6, 7, 8, 9, 10]
```

Puzzle 15

```python
def filter_palindromes(input_strs: list[str]) -> list[str]:
    return [
        input_str
        for input_str in input_strs
        if input_str.lower() == input_str.lower()[::-1]
    ]
```

This solution uses a conditional list comprehension with the condition of "if the lowercase version of *input_str* is equal to the lowercase version of *input_str* reversed, return *True*".

Puzzle 16

```python
def censor_python(input_strs: list[str]) -> list[str]:
    censored_chars = ["P", "Y", "T", "H", "O", "N"]
    return [
        "".join(
            ["X" if char.upper() in censored_chars else char
                for char in input_str]
        ) for input_str in input_strs
    ]
```

This solution can be broken up into the following steps:

1. Initialise the *censored_chars* list with the characters that need to be censored: "P", "Y", "T", "H", "O", and "N".

2. Start a list comprehension that iterates over each input string (*input_str*) in the *input_strs* list.

3. For each input string, start an inner list comprehension that iterates over each character (*char*) in the string.

4. Check if the uppercase version of the character (*char.upper()*) is found in the *censored_chars* list.

5. If the character is found in *censored_chars*, replace it with the letter "X", else keep the original character.

6. Join the modified characters back together to form a new string using the *"".join()* function.

7. Collect the modified string for each input string into a new list.

8. Return the resulting list.

Puzzle 17

```python
def check_if_string_is_happy(input_str: str) -> bool:
    return not any(
        a == b or a == c or b == c
        for a, b, c in
            zip(input_str, input_str[1:], input_str[2:])
    )
```

This solution can be broken up into the following steps:

1. The code uses the *zip()* function to iterate over three consecutive characters in *input_str* simultaneously. It pairs up each character (*a*) with the next character (*b*) and the character after that (*c*).

2. The code then uses a generator expression within the *any()* function to check if any of the characters are equal to each other.

3. The *any()* function returns *True* if any of the comparisons in the generator expression evaluate to *True*, and *False* otherwise.

4. The result is then negated and returned.

Puzzle 18

```python
def get_number_of_digits(input_num: int) -> int:
    if input_num // 10 == 0:
        return 1
    return 1 + get_number_of_digits(input_num // 10)
```

This solution makes use of recursion to calculate the result, here's how it works:

1. The first if statement returns 1 if *input_num* divided by 10 (using integer division //) is equal to 0. This condition is *True* when *input_num* has only one digit.

2. If the above condition is not met, the code executes the recursive step. It calls the *get_number_of_digits* function again with *input_num* // *10* as the argument. This recursively integer divides *input_num* by 10, effectively removing the rightmost digit.

3. The result of the recursive call is then incremented by 1 before being returned. This increment accounts for the current digit being counted in the total number of digits.

4. The recursion continues until the base case (first if statement) is satisfied and the recursive calls unwind.

Puzzle 19

```python
def get_tic_tac_toe_winner(input_board: list[list[str]])
        -> str | None:

    # Check rows
    for row in input_board:
        if row[0] == row[1] == row[2]:
            return row[0]

    # Check columns
    for i in range(3):
        if input_board[0][i] == input_board[1][i]
            == input_board[2][i]:
            return input_board[0][i]

    # Check diagonals
    if input_board[0][0] == input_board[1][1]
        == input_board[2][2]:
        return input_board[0][0]
    if input_board[0][2] == input_board[1][1]
        == input_board[2][0]:
        return input_board[0][2]

    return None
```

This solution performs four checks:

1. Three in a row horizontally by iterating over each row and seeing if the first three elements are equal

2. Three in a column vertically by checking each column at the first, second and third row

3. Top left to bottom right diagonal

4. Bottom left to top right diagonal

If none of the if statements return a character then the game is a draw so *None* is returned.

Puzzle 20

```
def print_triangle(number_of_levels: int, symbol: str) -> None:
    for level in range(1, number_of_levels + 1):
        print(" "
            * (number_of_levels - level) + symbol
            * (2 * level - 1)
        )
```

This solution makes use of a print statement inside of a for loop to generate each level, here is how the print is broken up:

- The first part of the string is created using " " *
  (number_of_levels - level). This generates a string of spaces
  based on the difference between the total number of levels
  (number_of_levels) and the current level *(level)*. This creates the
  indentation for each level, so that higher levels are more indented
  than lower levels.

- The second part of the string is constructed using *symbol* * *(2* *
  level - 1). This generates a string of the specified symbol
  repeated *(2* * *level - 1)* times. The formula *2* * *level - 1*
  calculates the number of symbols in each level, where the first level
  has 1 symbol, the second level has 3 symbols, the third level has 5
  symbols, and so on.

Puzzle 21

```
def fibonacci(sequence_number: int) -> int:
    if sequence_number in (0, 1):
        return sequence_number
    return fibonacci(sequence_number - 1)
        + fibonacci(sequence_number - 2)
```

This solution can be broken up into two parts:

1. The base case: if the *sequence_number* is 0 or 1 we return this value as it's the beginning of the fibonacci sequence - *fibonacci(0) = 0 and fibonacci(1) = 1.*

2. The function makes a recursive call to itself twice, with sequence_number - 1 and *sequence_number - 2* as the arguments. The result of the recursive calls are summed together when the base case is reached and we start moving back up the stack.

Puzzle 22

```
def harmonic_sum(n: int) -> float:
    if n < 2:
        return 1
    return 1 / n + harmonic_sum(n - 1)
```

This solution can be broken up into three parts:

1. The base case: if *n* is less than 2, we return 1 as *harmonic_sum(0)* = *1 and harmonic_sum(1)* = *1*.

2. The function makes a recursive call to itself with *n* - *1* as the argument. This recursive call calculates the harmonic sum for the preceding value of *n*. The recursive calls continue until they reach the base case, at which point they start returning values back up the call stack.

3. Once the recursive calls reach the base case, the function starts calculating the harmonic sum by adding the reciprocal of *n* to the result of the recursive call. Once the recursive stack is empty the final harmonic sum value is returned.

Puzzle 23

```python
def xor(input_a: str, input_b: str) -> str:
    result = ""
    for i in range(min(len(input_a), len(input_b))):
        if input_a[i] == input_b[i]:
            result += "0"
        else:
            result += "1"
    return result
```

This solution works by iterating through the characters in *input_a* and *input_b* using a for loop. For each pair of characters, it checks if they are the same or different. If they are the same, it adds a 0 to the result string. If they are different, it adds a 1 to the result string.

Puzzle 24

```python
from typing import Any

def my_zip(input_list_a: list[Any], input_list_b: list[Any])
    -> list[tuple[Any, Any]]:

    zipped_result = []
    for i in range(min(len(input_list_a), len(input_list_b))):
        zipped_result.append(
            (input_list_a[i], input_list_b[i])
        )
    return zipped_result
```

This solution first initialises an empty list named *zipped_result* that will store the resulting tuples.

We then use a for loop to loop through every index of the shortest list, the index number is denoted by the variable *i*. By looping through the shortest list we ensure the loop only iterates up to the length of the shorter list to avoid an *IndexError* if the lists have different lengths.

Inside the loop, the function appends a tuple to the *zipped_result* list. The tuple contains the element at index *i* from *input_list_a* paired with the element at the same index *i* from *input_list_b*.

Once the loop has finished we return the result.

Puzzle 25

```python
def is_valid_equation(input_equation: str) -> bool:
    try:
        left_num, operator, right_num, _, result_num
            = input_equation.split()

        if operator == "+":
            return int(left_num) + int(right_num)
                == int(result_num)
        if operator == "-":
            return int(left_num) - int(right_num)
                == int(result_num)
        return False
    except ValueError:
        return False
```

This solution first splits up the *input_equation* by spaces. Each part of the equation from the split is then loaded into the representative variables, we've loaded the "equals" part of the equation into a variable with the name "_" as we don't need this value.

We then have two if statements, one for if the operator is a plus and one for if it's a minus. If the condition of either of these if statements is *True* then we calculate the expression and check both sides of the equation are equal.

If the operator isn't a plus or minus we return *False*. If a *ValueError* occurs during the execution of the code within the try block, it means that the input equation could not be properly split into the expected components. In this case, the except block is executed, and the function returns *False*.

Puzzle 26

```python
from typing import Any

def rotate_list_left(input_list: list[Any], rotate_amount: int)
    -> list[Any]:

    rotate_amount %= len(input_list)

    return input_list[rotate_amount:]
        + input_list[:rotate_amount]
```

This solution returns the result of concatenating two slices of the *input_list* using the + operator:

1. Firstly we use the modulo operator to reduce the *rotate_amount* so it's less than the size of our list. This is working on the principle that if we have a list of length 5, and rotate it 5 times, we have the same list. So if we have a list of length 5 and a *rotate_amount* of 7, we can say the rotate amount is 2.

2. Then onto the slicing, the first slice *input_list[rotate_amount:]*, represents the elements of *input_list* starting from the *rotate_amount* index up to the end of the list. This slice captures the elements that need to be moved to the front of the list during the rotation.

3. The second slice, *input_list[:rotate_amount]*, represents the elements of *input_list* from the beginning of the list up to the *rotate_amount* index. This slice captures the elements that need to be moved to the end of the list during the rotation.

By concatenating these two slices, the function effectively rotates the elements of the *input_list* *rotate_amount* positions to the left.

Puzzle 27

```
def find_adjacent_nodes(
    adj_matrix: list[list[int]],
    start_node: int
) -> list[int]:

    return [i for i, is_connected in
        enumerate(adj_matrix[start_node]) if is_connected]
```

You might be surprised the solution for this puzzle is just one line, but there is actually a lot happening! Here's how it works:

1. The code uses a list comprehension to iterate over each element in the *adj_matrix[start_node]* list. This sublist represents the row in the adjacency matrix corresponding to the *start_node*.

2. Within the list comprehension, each element is represented by the variables i and *is_connected*. The variable i stores the index of the current element, and *is_connected* contains the true (1) or false (0) value indicating if the node is connected to another node.

3. The list comprehension condition if *is_connected* filters out elements that are not connected to the *start_node*. This condition will only be true if *is_connected* is not equal to 0.

4. The filtered elements are collected in a new list created by the list comprehension, effectively creating a list of indices representing the adjacent nodes connected to the *start_node*.

5. Finally, the list of adjacent nodes is returned as the result of the function.

Puzzle 28

```python
def count_peaks_valleys(price_action: list[int])
    -> tuple[int, int]:

    peaks = 0
    valleys = 0
    for price_idx in range(1, len(price_action) - 1):
        if (
            price_action[price_idx - 1]
            < price_action[price_idx]
            > price_action[price_idx + 1]
        ):
            peaks += 1
        elif (
            price_action[price_idx - 1]
            > price_action[price_idx]
            < price_action[price_idx + 1]
        ):
            valleys += 1
    return peaks, valleys
```

This solution loops through the *price_action* list from the second value to the second from last value. Inside of the loop we have two conditions:

1. To detect a peak the following conditions must evaluate to *True*:

    a. The price before the current price must be less than the current price

    b. The price after the current price must be more than the current price

2. To detect a valley the following conditions must evaluate to *True*:

    a. The price before the current price must be more than the current price

    b. The price after the current price must be less than the current price

If a peak or valley is detected we then increment the *peaks* or *valleys* counters and return these counters when the loop has finished.

Puzzle 29

```python
tap_code_map = {
    "a": ". .",          "b": ". ..",          "c": ". ...",
    "d": ". ....",       "e": ". .....",       "f": ".. ..",
    "g": ".. ...",       "h": ".. ....",       "i": ".. .....",
    "j": ".. ......",    "l": "... ..",        "m": "... ...",
    "n": "... ....",     "o": "... .....",     "p": "... ......",
    "q": ".... ..",      "r": ".... ...",      "s": ".... ....",
    "t": ".... ....","u": ".... .....",        "v": "..... ..",
    "w": "..... ...",    "x": "..... ....",    "y": "..... .....",
    "z": "..... ....."
}


def tap_code_to_english(input_code: str) -> str:
    tap_code_map_inv = {v: k for k, v in tap_code_map.items()}

    if len(input_code) == 0:
        return ""

    # Break up the tap code into separate words, convert each
    # word and then concatenate the result together

    words_as_tap_code = input_code.split("  ")
    return " ".join(
        [
            "".join(
                tap_code_map_inv[letter_as_tap_code]
                for letter_as_tap_code
                    in word_as_tap_code.split("  ")
            )
            for word_as_tap_code in words_as_tap_code
        ]
    )
```

This solution starts off by switching the order of the *tap_code_map* so that
the values become keys and the keys become values. We could have
defined the map the other way round in the first place however it's easier to
look at with the letters as keys and the tap code as values.

We then have a simple check to return an empty string if the length of *input_code* is 0.

Here we get to the main part of processing, we first split the input code into a list of tap code words (remember a word in tap code is split by three spaces). Once we have our list of tap code words we process it as follows:

1. Inside of a list comprehension, for each tap code word:

    a. Split the tap code word into a list of tap code letters (remember a letter in tap code is split by two spaces).

    b. Look up the letter equivalent of the tap code using *tap_code_map_inv*.

    c. Join the converted letters.

2. Join the returned list from the list comprehension with a space in between to produce the converted result.

Puzzle 30

```python
def find_zero_sum_triplets(input_nums: list[int])
    -> list[tuple[int, int, int]]:

    zero_sum_triplets = []

    for i in range(len(input_nums)):
        for j in range(i + 1, len(input_nums)):
            for k in range(j + 1, len(input_nums)):
                if input_nums[i] + input_nums[j]
                    + input_nums[k] == 0:
                    zero_sum_triplets.append((i, j, k))

    return zero_sum_triplets
```

This solution starts off by initialising an empty list called *zero_sum_triplets* that is used to store the resulting triplets. The code uses three nested for loops to iterate over all possible combinations of three different elements from the *input_nums* list:

1. The outer loop, controlled by the variable *i*, iterates over the indices of *input_nums* from 0 to the length of the list.

2. The middle loop, controlled by the variable *j*, iterates over the indices starting from *i + 1* to the length of the list. This ensures that *j* will always be greater than *i*, preventing duplicate combinations.

3. The innermost loop, controlled by the variable *k*, iterates over the indices starting from *j + 1* to the length of the list. This ensures that *k* will always be greater than both *i* and *j*, again preventing duplicate combinations.

Within the innermost loop, the code checks if the sum of the elements at indices *i*, *j*, and *k* in the *input_nums* list is equal to zero. If the sum is zero, it means a triplet has been found whose sum is zero. In that case, a tuple *(i, j, k)* representing the indices of the three elements is appended to the *zero_sum_triplets* list.

After all the iterations, the function returns the *zero_sum_triplets* list containing all the found triplets.

Puzzle 31

```python
from typing import Any

def param_count(*args: Any) -> int:
    return len(args)
```

This solution defines a function called *param_count* that takes in a variable number of arguments using the *args* syntax. The function returns the length of the *args* tuple using the *Len* function.

Puzzle 31.1 - Bonus Solution

There are two different approaches to the bonus task. The first solution will likely be closer to what you've written as it's what first comes to mind. The second solution makes use of iterables and is closer to how python actually implements the *zip* function.

```python
from typing import Any

def my_zip(*input_lists: list[Any]) -> list[tuple[Any, ...]]:
    if len(input_lists) == 0:
        return []

    shortest_length = min(len(input_list) for input_list
        in input_lists)
    zipped_result = [tuple() for _ in range(shortest_length)]

    for i in range(shortest_length):
        for input_list in input_lists:
            zipped_result[i] += (input_list[i],)

    return zipped_result
```

This solution can be broken up into five parts:

1. If *input_lists* is empty, return an empty list.

2. Calculate the length of the shortest list in *input_lists* making use of the *min* and *Len* functions along with a generator expression.

3. Create a list of empty tuples where the number of tuples in the list is equal to the length of the shortest input list.

4. Create an outer loop ranging from 0 to the length of shortest list:

    a. Inside the loop, loop over each of the *input_lists* and add the i-th element to the i-th resulting tuple

b. Here we make use of tuple addition, for example:

    i.   If *zipped_result[i]* = *(1, 2, 3)*

    ii.   And we execute *zipped_result[i]* += *(4,)*

    iii. Then the resulting tuple will be *(1, 2, 3, 4)*

5. Finally we return the result.

Puzzle 31.1 - Alternative Bonus Solution

```python
from typing import Any
from collections.abc import Iterator

def my_zip(*input_lists: list[Any])
    -> Iterator[tuple[Any, ...]]:

    sentinel = object()
    input_lists_iterators = [
        iter(input_list) for input_list in input_lists
    ]
    while input_lists_iterators:
        zipped_result = []
        for input_list_iterator in input_lists_iterators:
            elem = next(input_list_iterator, sentinel)
            if elem is sentinel:
                return
            zipped_result.append(elem)
        yield tuple(zipped_result)
```

This solution is a closer implementation of how Python's *zip* function works. Here's what's happening:

1. A *sentinel* object is created. This object will be used to detect when an input list has been exhausted.

2. For each input list in *input_lists*, an iterator is created using the *iter()* function. This iterator will allow us to iterate over the elements of each input list.

3. The function enters a while loop, which continues until all input list iterators are exhausted:

    a. Within the loop, a new empty list called *zipped_result* is created.

b. For each input list iterator in *input_lists_iterators*, the function attempts to retrieve the next element using *next(input_list_iterator, sentinel)*.

    i. If there is a next element, it is appended to the *zipped_result* list.

    ii. If the iterator is exhausted (i.e., *next()* returns the *sentinel* object), the function exits early using the return statement.

c. After iterating over all input list iterators, a tuple is created from the elements in *zipped_result* using the *tuple()* function.

d. The tuple is yielded using the *yield* statement, which allows the function to produce a generator of tuples. This means that the function can be iterated over to obtain the tuples one at a time.

4. If all input list iterators are exhausted, the function completes, and no further tuples are generated.

Puzzle 32

```python
def contains_python_chars(input_str: str) -> bool:
    input_str = input_str.lower()
    python_chars = set("python")

    for i in range(len(input_str) - len(python_chars) + 1):
        if set(input_str[i:i + len(python_chars)])
            == python_chars:
            return True
    return False
```

This solution first converts the input string to lowercase using the *Lower* function so that the function is case-insensitive. Then it checks whether the string contains any permutation of the word python.

1. A set called *python_chars* is created with the characters "python". This will be used for comparisons later.

2. The function enters a for loop ranging from 0 to the length of *input_str* minus the length of *python_chars* + *1*. This ensures that we don't go out of bounds when slicing the *input_str* inside of the loop.

   a. Inside the loop, a substring of *input_str* starting from index *i* and with a length equal to the length of *python_chars* is extracted using slicing: *input_str[i:i + Len(python_chars)]*.

   b. The extracted substring is converted to a set using the *set()* function and then compared with the *python_chars* set using the == operator.

   c. If the two sets are equal, it means that the substring contains all the characters "python" and *True* is returned.

   d. If none of the substrings match the *python_chars* set, the loop continues until all possible substrings have been checked.

3. If the loop completes without finding a match, the function returns *False* to indicate that *input_str* does not contain "python".

Puzzle 33

```python
def is_prime(input_num: int) -> bool:
    if input_num < 2:
        return False

    for i in range(2, input_num):
        if input_num % i == 0:
            return False
    return True


def find_primes(input_nums: list[int]) -> list[int]:
    return [input_num for input_num in input_nums
        if is_prime(input_num)]
```

This solution defines a helper function *is_prime* that takes an integer and returns *True* if the integer is prime, and *False* otherwise. The *find_primes* function uses list comprehension and the *is_prime* function to create a new list containing only the prime numbers from the input list.

Puzzle 34

```python
def rot13(input_str: str) -> str:
    result = ""

    for char in input_str:
        if char.isalpha():
            a_code = ord("A") if char.isupper() else ord("a")
            char = chr((ord(char) - a_code + 13) % 26 + a_code)

        result += char

    return result
```

This solution starts off by initialising an empty string called *result*, it then loop over the *input_str*:

1. Within the loop, an if statement checks if the *char* is alphabetic using the *isalpha* method. If the character is alphabetic, the function proceeds to perform the ROT13 transformation on it.

2. Inside the if block, the variable *a_code* is set to the ASCII code of either uppercase "A" or lowercase "a" based on the case of the current character.

3. The ROT13 transformation is applied to the character, let's break down this line:

    a. *ord(char)*: The *ord()* function is used to get the ASCII code of *char*.

    b. *(ord(char) - a_code + 13)*: Here, the ASCII code of the character is subtracted by the value of *a_code*. This step is performed to normalise the character's value relative to the starting point of the alphabet (either uppercase or lowercase).

c. **% 26**: The resulting value from the previous step is then taken modulo 26. This operation ensures that the value wraps around within the range of the 26 letters of the alphabet. It effectively handles cases where the subtraction goes beyond the alphabet's range.

d. **+ a_code**: After taking the modulo 26, the value is added back to *a_code*. This step adjusts the value to the correct ASCII code range of either uppercase or lowercase letters.

e. **chr(...)**: Finally, the resulting adjusted ASCII code is converted back to a character using the *chr()* function. This produces the transformed character based on the ROT13 cipher.

4. The loop continues until all characters in *input_str* have been processed and then the *result* is returned.

Example

The confusing part to this solution is the *char = chr((ord(char) - a_code + 13) % 26 + a_code)* line, so let's take a look at an example for further clarification:

```
char = "Y"
a_code = ord("A") = 65

chr((ord(char) - a_code + 13) % 26 + a_code)
 = chr((89 - 65 + 13) % 26 + a_code)  # Evaluated ord(char) and a_code
 = chr(37 % 26 + a_code)              # Evaluated (89 - 65 + 13) = 37
 = chr(11 + a_code)                   # Evaluated 37 % 26 = 11
 = chr(11 + 65)                       # Evaluated a_code
 = chr(76)                            # Evaluated 11 + 65 = 76
 = "L"                                # Evaluated chr(76) = "L"
```

Puzzle 35

```python
def get_parentheses_groups(input_str: str) -> list[str]:
    open_indices = []
    groups = []
    start_index = 0

    for i, char in enumerate(input_str):
        if char == "(":
            open_indices.append(i)
        elif char == ")":
            if open_indices:
                open_indices.pop()
                if not open_indices:
                    group = input_str[start_index:i + 1]
                        .replace(" ", "")
                    groups.append(group)
                    start_index = i + 1
    return groups
```

1. The solution starts off by initialising three variables:

    a. An empty list called *open_indices*, which will store the indices of opening parentheses encountered.

    b. An empty list called *groups* which will hold the extracted groups of parentheses.

    c. The variable *start_index* which is initialised at 0. It represents the starting index of the current group.

2. The function enters a for loop that iterates over each *char* in *input_str* along with its corresponding index *i*. The loop body is split into two conditions:

    a. If *char* is equal to "(":

        i. The *i* index is appended to the *open_indices* list.

    b. If the *char* is equal to ")":

    i.   If there are previously encountered open parentheses (*open_indices* is not empty), the most recent open parenthesis index is removed from *open_indices* using *open_indices.pop()*. This indicates a matching closing parenthesis has been found.

    ii.   If, after removing the open parenthesis index, the *open_indices* list becomes empty, it means that a complete group of parentheses has been found. In this case we:

        1. Slice the group of brackets out of the input string and remove any spaces between them.

        2. Append the resulting group of brackets to the *groups* list.

        3. Set the start index to $i + 1$, indicating the start index of the next group.

3. Once the loop has finished we return the resulting *groups* list.

Puzzle 36

```
def matrix_multiply(
    left_matrix: list[list[int]], right_matrix: list[list[int]]
) -> list[list[int]]:

    num_left_rows = len(left_matrix)
    num_left_cols = len(left_matrix[0])
    num_right_cols = len(right_matrix[0])

    if num_left_rows != num_right_cols:
        return None

    result_matrix = [[0 for _ in range(num_right_cols)]
        for _ in range(num_left_rows)]

    for i in range(num_left_rows):
        for k in range(num_left_cols):
            for j in range(num_right_cols):
                result_matrix[i][j]
                    += left_matrix[i][k] * right_matrix[k][j]

    return result_matrix
```

This solution works as follows:

1. The function first determines the dimensions of the left and right matrices:

    a. *num_left_rows* is set to the number of rows in the left matrix, obtained using *len(left_matrix)*.

    b. *num_left_cols* is set to the number of columns in the left matrix, obtained using *len(left_matrix[0])*.

    c. *num_right_cols* is set to the number of columns in the right matrix, obtained using *len(right_matrix[0])*.

2. If the matrix can't be multiplied because *num_left_rows !=* *num_right_cols* then we return *None*.

3. A result matrix is initialised as a nested list of zeros using list comprehension:

    a. The dimensions of the *result_matrix* are *num_left_rows x num_right_cols*

4. The function enters three nested for loops to perform the matrix multiplication:

    a. The outer loop iterates over the rows of the left matrix using the variable *i*.

    b. The middle loop iterates over the columns of the left matrix and rows of the right matrix using the variable *k*.

    c. The innermost loop iterates over the columns of the right matrix using the variable *j*. Inside the innermost loop, the elements of the resulting matrix are calculated:

        i. The element at position *[i][j]* of the resulting matrix is updated by adding the product of the corresponding elements from the left and right matrices.

5. After all the iterations, the resulting matrix, which holds the matrix multiplication result, is returned.

Puzzle 37

```python
def gcd(num_one: int, num_two: int) -> int:
    if num_two == 0:
        return num_one
    return gcd(num_two, num_one % num_two)
```

This solution starts off by defining a base case: $if\ num\_two == 0$. If num_two is equal to 0, it means that num_one is the GCD of the two numbers since any number divided by 0 is equal to itself. In this case, the function immediately returns num_one.

If the base case condition is not met, the function recursively calls itself:

1. The function is called with the arguments num_two and num_one % num_two. This is done to calculate the GCD by recursively reducing the problem to a smaller instance.

2. The new arguments represent the previous num_two as the new num_one, and the remainder of num_one divided by num_two as the new num_two.

3. The recursion continues until num_two becomes 0 (as per the base case condition).

Once the base case is reached, the function returns the GCD, which is the value stored in num_one.

Example

```
gcd(10, 15)

gcd(15, 10 % 15)
 = gcd(15, 10)    # 10 % 15 = 10

gcd(10, 15 % 10)
 = gcd(10, 5)     # 15 % 10 = 5

gcd(5, 10 % 5)
 = gcd(5, 0)      # Base case hit as num_two == 0
 = 5
```

Puzzle 38

```python
def find_pairs_summing_to_target(
    input_nums: list[int], target: int
) -> list[tuple[int, int]]:

    pairs = []

    for left_idx, left_num in enumerate(input_nums):
        for _, right_num in enumerate(
            input_nums[left_idx + 1:]
        ):

            if left_num + right_num == target:
                pairs.append((left_num, right_num))

    return pairs
```

The solution initialises an empty list called *pairs*. The function then enters a nested for loop:

1. The outer loop iterates over *input_nums* using the *enumerate* function to get both the index *left_idx* and the corresponding value *left_num*.

    a. The inner loop iterates over a slice of the *input_nums* list, starting from *left_idx + 1* onwards. This ensures that each pair is unique and avoids repetitions.

    b. Inside the inner loop, the sum of *left_num* and *right_num* is checked against the *target* value. If the sum is equal we append a *(left_num, right_num)* tuple to the *pairs* list.

After both loops have finished iterating, the function returns the *pairs* list containing all the pairs of numbers that sum up to the *target*.

Puzzle 38.1 - Bonus Solution

```python
def find_pairs_summing_to_target_bonus(
    input_nums: list[int], target: int
) -> list[tuple[int, int]]:

    pairs = set()
    seen = set()

    for input_num in input_nums:

        if target - input_num in seen:
            pairs.add((input_num, target - input_num))
        else:
            seen.add(input_num)

    return list(pairs)
```

This solution uses a single for loop and a set to achieve *O(n)* time complexity, which is more efficient than the solution using nested for loops. Here's how it works:

1. We start off by initialising two variables:

    a. An empty set called *pairs* to store the pairs of numbers that sum up to *target*.

    b. An empty set called *seen* to keep track of the numbers that have been encountered while iterating through *input_nums*.

2. The function then enters a loop where it iterates over each *input_num* in the *input_nums* list:

    a. For each *input_num*, it checks if the difference between *target* and *input_num* is present in the *seen* set. If the difference is present in the *seen* set, it means there is a pair of numbers that sum up to the *target*. In this case, we add a tuple *(input_num, target - input_num)* to the *pairs* set.

b. If the difference is not present in the *seen* set, it means the current *input_num* does not have a pair that sums up to *target* yet. In this case, it adds the *input_num* to the *seen* set for future reference.

3. The loop continues until all *input_nums* have been processed and finally returns the *pairs* set, casted to a list.

Puzzle 39

```python
def tower_of_hanoi(num_disks: int, source: str, aux: str,
target: str)
    -> None:

    if num_disks > 0:

        tower_of_hanoi(num_disks - 1, source, target, aux)
        print(f"Move disk {num_disks} from {source} to {target}")
        tower_of_hanoi(num_disks - 1, aux, source, target)
```

This solution makes use of recursively calling itself twice to solve the problem, lets see how it works:

1. The base case for the recursion is defined: if *num_disks* is greater than 0, the recursion continues. Otherwise, if *num_disks* is 0 or negative, the function returns without performing any further operations.

2. Inside the function, a recursive call is made to *tower_of_hanoi* with *num_disks* - 1 disks. Note that the roles of the *aux* and *target* towers are swapped in this recursive call.

3. After the recursive call, the line *print(f"Move disk {num_disks} from {source} to {target}")* is executed.

4. Another recursive call is made to *tower_of_hanoi* with *num_disks* - 1 disks, but this time the roles of the *source* and *aux* towers are swapped. This step ensures that the remaining disks on the *aux* tower are moved to the *target* tower, using the *source* tower as an auxiliary.

By following these steps, the Tower of Hanoi algorithm recursively moves the disks from the source tower to the target tower, using the auxiliary tower as a temporary storage, while ensuring that no larger disk is placed on top of a smaller disk.

Puzzle 40

```python
def insertion_sort(input_nums: list[int]) -> list[int]:
    for key_index in range(1, len(input_nums)):
        value_to_insert = input_nums[key_index]
        previous_index = key_index - 1

        while previous_index >= 0 \
            and value_to_insert < input_nums[previous_index]:

            input_nums[previous_index + 1] = \
                input_nums[previous_index]

            previous_index -= 1

        input_nums[previous_index + 1] = value_to_insert

    return input_nums
```

This solution makes use of a for loop to sort the list, here's how it works:

1. The for loop iterates over the range from index 1 to the length of the *input_nums* list. This means it's starting with the second element of the list.

2. Inside the loop, the value of the element at the current *key_index* is stored in the variable *value_to_insert*.

3. The variable *previous_index* is set to *key_index - 1*, representing the index of the element before the current one.

4. A while loop is used to compare the *value_to_insert* with the elements before it (starting from the previous index) and shifts them to the right if they are greater than *value_to_insert*. The loop continues as long as *previous_index* is greater than or equal to 0 and the element at *previous_index* is greater than *value_to_insert*.

a. Inside the while loop, the element at *previous_index* is
    moved one position to the right
    (*input_nums[previous_index + 1]* =
    input_nums[previous_index]). This creates a space for
    the *value_to_insert* to be placed in the correct sorted
    position.

b. The *previous_index* is decremented by 1 to move to the
    next element towards the beginning of the list.

5. Once the while loop ends, the correct position for *value_to_insert*
    is found, and it is assigned to *input_nums[previous_index + 1]*.

6. The for loop continues to the next element, repeating the process
    until all elements have been processed.

Finally, the sorted *input_nums* list is returned as the output of the function.

Puzzle 41

```python
roman_map = { 1000: "M", 900: "CM", 500: "D", 400: "CD",
100: "C", 90: "XC", 50: "L", 40: "XL", 10: "X", 9: "IX",
5: "V", 4: "IV", 1: "I" }


def int_to_roman(input_num: int) -> str:
    result = ""

    for roman_int_value in sorted(
        roman_map.keys(), reverse=True
    ):
        while input_num >= roman_int_value:
            result += roman_map[roman_int_value]
            input_num -= roman_int_value

    return result
```

We start off by initialising an empty *result* string, this will store the converted value.

A for loop is then used to iterate over the keys of the *roman_map* dictionary in descending order. This ensures that the largest possible Roman numeral values are considered first.

Inside the for loop, a while loop is used which will:

1. Append the *roman_map[roman_int_value]* to the result using string concatenation (*result += roman_map[roman_int_value]*).

2. Decrement the current *roman_int_value* to reduce the remaining value that needs to be converted.

Once the while loop ends, the code moves to the next iteration of the for loop, considering the next smaller *roman_int_value*.

Once the loops have finished, the result is returned.

Puzzle 41.1 - Bonus Solution

```python
roman_map = { 1000: "M", 900: "CM", 500: "D", 400: "CD",
100: "C", 90: "XC", 50: "L", 40: "XL", 10: "X", 9: "IX",
5: "V", 4: "IV", 1: "I" }

def roman_to_int(input_str: str) -> int:
    roman_map_swapped = {v: k for k, v in roman_map.items()}
    result = 0
    prev_value = 0

    for char in input_str:
        value = roman_map_swapped[char]
        if value > prev_value:
            result -= prev_value
            result += value - prev_value
        else:
            result += value

        prev_value = value

    return result
```

For the first part of this solution we define the *roman_to_int* function. This function works as follows:

1. A new dictionary *roman_map_swapped* is created by swapping the keys and values of *roman_map*. We do this so we can use the roman numeral values as keys.

2. Initialise the variable *result* as 0. This variable will store the resulting value.

3. Initialise the variable *prev_value* as 0. This variable keeps track of the previous integer value encountered during the iteration.

4. A for loop iterates over each character in the *input_str* string, inside the loop we:

    a. Retrieve the integer value of the current Roman numeral by looking it up in the *roman_map_swapped* dictionary.

    b. Check if the *value* is greater than the *prev_value*. This comparison determines whether the current Roman numeral represents a subtractive or additive combination.

        i. If *value* is greater than *prev_value* we subtract *prev_value* from *result* and add the difference between *value* and *prev_value* to *result*. This subtraction accounts for the subtractive combination of Roman numerals (e.g., IV = 4, CM = 900).

        ii. If *value* is not greater than *prev_value* we add the value directly to *result*. This addition accounts for the additive combination of Roman numerals (e.g., VI = 6, XI = 11).

    c. Update *prev_value* to *value* for the next iteration.

Finally, the *result* variable is returned as the output of the function.

```
def int_roman_converter(to_convert: str | int) -> int | str:
    # roman numerals to int
    if isinstance(to_convert, str):
        return roman_to_int(to_convert)

    # int to roman numerals
    if isinstance(to_convert, int):
        return int_to_roman(to_convert)

    return None
```

The *int_roman_converter* is the final piece of the puzzle, we work on the assumption that if *to_convert* is of type *str* then we want to convert from roman numerals to *int* and if *to_convert* is of type *int* we want to convert from *int* to roman numerals.

If *to_convert* isn't of type *str* or *int* we simply return *None*.

Puzzle 42

```python
def bitwise_add(num_one: int, num_two: int) -> int:
    while num_two != 0:
        carry = num_one & num_two
        num_one = num_one ^ num_two
        num_two = carry << 1

    return num_one
```

This solution utilises a while loop to handle the carry bits in the addition process, inside the loop the code performs the following operations:

1. It calculates the carry by performing a bitwise AND operation (&) between *num_one* and *num_two* and assigns the result to the variable *carry*.

2. It updates *num_one* by performing a bitwise XOR operation (^) between *num_one* and *num_two*. This step adds the two numbers without considering any carry.

3. It updates *num_two* by shifting the value of carry one position to the left (*carry* << 1). Shifting the *carry* left by one position prepares it to be added in the next iteration.

Once *num_two* becomes zero, the loop exits, and the final result is stored in *num_one*. This represents the sum of the two input numbers. The function returns *num_one* as the result of the addition.

To explain further, it's easier to visualise in an example:

```
num_one = 9 (binary: 1001)
num_two = 5 (binary: 0101)

Start the while loop:

Iteration 1:
carry = num_one & num_two = 1001 & 0101 = 0001 (carry: 1)
num_one = num_one ^ num_two = 1001 ^ 0101 = 1100 (num_one: 12)
num_two = carry << 1 = 0001 << 1 = 0010 (num_two: 2)

Iteration 2:
carry = num_one & num_two = 1100 & 0010 = 0000 (carry: 0)
num_one = num_one ^ num_two = 1100 ^ 0010 = 1110 (num_one: 14)
num_two = carry << 1 = 0000 << 1 = 0000 (num_two: 0)
```

Exit the while loop since num_two is now 0. The final result is num_one, which is 14.

Puzzle 43

```python
def binary_search(sorted_list: list[int], value_to_find: int)
    -> int:

    low, mid = 0, 0
    high = len(sorted_list) - 1

    while low <= high:
        mid = (high + low) // 2
        # If value_to_find is greater, ignore left half
        if value_to_find > sorted_list[mid]:
            low = mid + 1
        # If value_to_find is smaller, ignore right half
        elif value_to_find < sorted_list[mid]:
            high = mid - 1
        # value_to_find is present at mid
        else:
            return mid
    # If we reach here, then the element was not present
    return -1
```

There are two ways to implement a binary search, recursively and iteratively. Both solutions have the same time complexity of $O(log\ n)$, however the iterative solution has a space complexity of $O(1)$ compared to the recursive version with a space complexity of $O(log\ n)$.

The solution makes use of three main variables Low, mid and $high$. While Low is less than or equal to $high$ we carry out the following steps:

1. Calculate mid as ($high + Low$) integer divided by 2.

2. Check if the value to find is greater than the mid index of our input list, if it is then ignore the left half of the list.

3. Check if the value to find is smaller than the mid index of our input list, if it is then ignore the right half of the list.

4. If the value to find isn't greater or smaller it means we've located it, so return the mid index.

If the loop ends without returning a value it means the value isn't present in the list, in this case we return -1.

Puzzle 44

```python
def quicksort(input_list: list[int], low: int, high: int)
    -> list[int]:

    if low < high:
        pivot_idx = partition(input_list, low, high)
        quicksort(input_list, low, pivot_idx - 1)
        quicksort(input_list, pivot_idx + 1, high)

    return input_list

def partition(input_list: list[int], low: int, high: int)
    -> int:

    pivot = input_list[high]
    pivot_idx = low - 1

    for current_idx in range(low, high):

        if input_list[current_idx] <= pivot:
            pivot_idx = pivot_idx + 1
            input_list[pivot_idx], input_list[current_idx] = (
                input_list[current_idx],
                input_list[pivot_idx],
            )

    input_list[pivot_idx + 1], input_list[high] = (
        input_list[high],
        input_list[pivot_idx + 1],
    )

    return pivot_idx + 1
```

In this solution the quicksort function is the main function that performs the sorting. It takes as input a list and two indices: *Low* and *high* that specify the portion of the list that needs to be sorted. The function uses the partition function to partition the list around a pivot element and then calls itself recursively to sort the two sub-lists on either side of the pivot.

The partition function implements the Lomuto partition scheme, which works as follows:

1. Choose the last element of the list as the pivot.

2. Initialise a variable $pivot\_idx$ to $Low - 1$.

3. Iterate over the elements $current\_idx$ in the range Low to $high - 1$.

4. If the element $input\_list[current\_idx]$ is less than or equal to the pivot, swap it with $input\_list[pivot\_idx + 1]$ and increment $pivot\_idx$ by 1.

5. After the loop, swap the pivot with $input\_list[pivot\_idx + 1]$.

6. Return $pivot\_idx + 1$ as the pivot index.

The partition function returns the index of the pivot element after partitioning the $input\_list$. The $quicksort$ function uses this index to determine the two sub-lists that need to be sorted in the next iteration. The algorithm terminates when $Low >= high$, which means that the sub-list has no more elements and is already sorted.

The average time complexity of this implementation is $O(n\ Log\ n)$, which makes it an efficient sorting algorithm for large lists. The space complexity of the implementation is $O(Log\ n)$ because it uses the divide-and-conquer approach, which requires only a logarithmic amount of extra space on the call stack.

As a tip, the best way to understand this solution is to step through it yourself. Set a breakpoint on the first line of the quicksort function and step through the code to see how it executes. Make your inputs as simple as possible so that execution doesn't get confusing.

Puzzle 45

```python
def solve_knapsack_problem(
    items: list[tuple[int, int]], knapsack_capacity: int
) -> int:
    # Start the recursive call from the last item
    return knapsack_recursive(
        items, len(items), knapsack_capacity
    )


def knapsack_recursive(
    items: list[tuple[int, int]],
    index: int,
    remaining_capacity: int
) -> int:
        # Base case: if we have considered all items or if the
        # capacity is zero
        if index == 0 or remaining_capacity == 0:
            return 0
        # Get the weight and value of the current item
        weight, value = items[index - 1]
        # If the current item's weight is more than the
        # remaining capacity, we can't include it
        if weight > remaining_capacity:
            return knapsack_recursive(
                items, index - 1, remaining_capacity
            )
        # Otherwise, we have two choices:
        # 1. Include the current item and recursively check the
        # remaining capacity
        include_current = value + knapsack_recursive(
            items, index - 1, remaining_capacity - weight
        )
        # 2. Exclude the current item and recursively check the
        # next item
        exclude_current = knapsack_recursive(
            items, index - 1, remaining_capacity
        )

        # Return the maximum value of the two choices
        return max(include_current, exclude_current)
```

This solution uses recursion to solve the knapsack problem, at each step of recursion the current item is either included or excluded from the knapsack. Once recursion is finished the maximum value will be returned.

Note: this recursive solution has a time complexity of $O(2^n)$ and therefore doesn't meet the requirements for puzzle 45.1 - Bonus.

Puzzle 45.1 - Bonus Solution

```python
def solve_knapsack_problem_bonus(
    items: list[tuple[int, int]], knapsack_capacity: int
) -> int:
    # Create a matrix to store the maximum value at each weight
    max_value_matrix = [
        [0 for _ in range(knapsack_capacity + 1)]
            for _ in range(len(items) + 1)]

    for item_idx in range(1, len(items) + 1):
        for weight in range(1, knapsack_capacity + 1):

            if items[item_idx - 1][0] > weight:
                max_value_matrix[item_idx][weight]
                    = max_value_matrix[item_idx - 1][weight]
            else:
                max_value_matrix[item_idx][weight] = max(
                    max_value_matrix[item_idx - 1][weight],
                    max_value_matrix[item_idx - 1]
                        [weight - items[item_idx - 1][0]]
                        + items[item_idx - 1][1],
                )

    return max_value_matrix[len(items)][knapsack_capacity]
```

The most time efficient algorithm for solving the knapsack problem is the dynamic programming algorithm, specifically the "bottom-up" approach. Let's take a look at how it works:

1. The code initialises a 2D matrix called *max_value_matrix* with dimensions *(len(items) + 1) x (knapsack_capacity + 1)*. This matrix will be used to store the maximum value that can be achieved at each weight. The matrix is initialised with zeros using list comprehension. Each row represents an item and each column represents a weight.

2. The code uses two nested loops to iterate over each item and weight combination, starting from the first item and a weight of 1.

3. Inside the nested loops, the code checks if the weight of the current item ($items[item\_idx - 1][0]$) is greater than the current weight being considered. If it is, it means the item cannot be included in the knapsack at this weight. Therefore, the maximum value remains the same as the previous item, so it is copied from the previous row of the matrix: $max\_value\_matrix[item\_idx][weight]$ = $max\_value\_matrix[item\_idx - 1][weight]$.

4. If the weight of the current item is less than or equal to the current weight being considered, it means the item can be included in the knapsack. In this case, the code calculates two values:

    a. The first value is the maximum value obtained by excluding the current item. This is taken from the previous row of the matrix: $max\_value\_matrix[item\_idx - 1][weight]$.

    b. The second value is the maximum value obtained by including the current item. It is calculated by adding the value of the current item ($items[item\_idx - 1][1]$) to the maximum value obtained at the weight difference ($weight - items[item\_idx - 1][0]$). This weight difference represents the remaining weight after including the current item.

    c. The maximum value of the two calculated values is assigned to $max\_value\_matrix[item\_idx][weight]$.

5. After iterating over all the items and weights, the function returns the maximum value stored in $max\_value\_matrix[len(items)][knapsack\_capacity]$, which represents the maximum value that can be achieved within the given weight constraint.

The time complexity of this algorithm is $O(nW)$, where n is the number of items and W is the maximum weight.

For further clarity, let's look at what a final matrix looks like for example inputs:

```
items = [(5, 2), (1, 1000), (100, 1), (25, 25), (2, 1000)]
Knapsack_capacity = 5

Max_value_matrix = [
     [0,    0,    0,    0,    0,    0],
     # At weight = 5 we can include (5, 2)
     [0,    0,    0,    0,    0,    2],
     # At weight >= 1 we can include (1, 1000)
     [0, 1000, 1000, 1000, 1000, 1000],
     # Can't include (100, 1) as weight > knapsack_capacity
     [0, 1000, 1000, 1000, 1000, 1000],
     # Can't include (25, 25) as weight > knapsack_capacity
     [0, 1000, 1000, 1000, 1000, 1000],
     # At weight >= 2 we can include (2, 1000)
     [0, 1000, 1000, 2000, 2000, 2000]  ]
```

- Each column of the matrix is representing a weight, with the first column being weight = 0, second weight = 1 etc.

- Each row of the matrix is representing an item with the first row being all 0s, second row being items[0], etc.

- To take the maximum possible value we return the bottom right value of the matrix.

Puzzle 46

```python
import socket
import struct

def ip_range_to_list(input_ip_range: str) -> list[str]:
    start, end = input_ip_range.split("-")
    start_ip = struct.unpack("!L", socket.inet_aton(start))[0]
    end_ip = struct.unpack("!L", socket.inet_aton(end))[0]
    return [
        socket.inet_ntoa(struct.pack("!L", ip_address))
        for ip_address in range(start_ip, end_ip + 1)
    ]
```

This solution uses the *split* method to separate the start and end IP addresses from the input string. It then uses *struct.unpack("!L", socket.inet_aton(ip))* to convert the IP addresses to 32-bit integers.

Then it uses list comprehension and *range(start_ip, end_ip + 1)* to generate a range of integers that correspond to the IP addresses within the range. *socket.inet_ntoa(struct.pack("!L", ip_address))* is then used to convert the integers back to IP addresses in the format "x.x.x.x"

This solution is more time efficient as it uses bitwise operations which are faster than string manipulation.

It is worth noting that this solution will only work for IPv4 addresses.

Let's look at an example for *input_ip_range = "192.168.1.1-192.168.1.5"*

```
start="192.168.1.1"
end="192.168.1.5"
start_ip = struct.unpack("!L", socket.inet_aton(start))[0]
  = struct.unpack("!L", b"\xc0\xa8\x01\x01")[0]
  = (3232235777,)[0]
  = 3232235777

end_ip = struct.unpack("!L", socket.inet_aton(end))[0]
  = struct.unpack("!L", b"\xc0\xa8\x01\x05")[0]
  = (3232235781,)[0]
  = 3232235781


[ socket.inet_ntoa(struct.pack("!L", ip_address))
     for ip_address in range(start_ip, end_ip + 1) ]

 = [socket.inet_ntoa(struct.pack("!L", ip_address))
     for ip_address in [3232235777, 3232235778, 3232235779,
                        3232235780, 3232235781]]

 = ["192.168.1.1", "192.168.1.2", "192.168.1.3", "192.168.1.4",
"192.168.1.5"]
```

Puzzle 47

```python
def solve_maze(
    maze: list[list[int]], start_pos: tuple[int, int], end_pos:
tuple[int, int]
) -> bool:

    num_rows, num_cols = len(maze), len(maze[0])
    queue = []
    queue.append(start_pos)
    maze[start_pos[1]][start_pos[0]] = 2

    while queue:
        curr_x, curr_y = queue.pop(0)

        if curr_x == end_pos[0] and curr_y == end_pos[1]:
            return True

        for exploring_x, exploring_y in [
            (curr_x + 1, curr_y),
            (curr_x - 1, curr_y),
            (curr_x, curr_y + 1),
            (curr_x, curr_y - 1),
        ]:
            if (
                0 <= exploring_x < num_cols
                and 0 <= exploring_y < num_rows
                and maze[exploring_y][exploring_x] == 0
            ):
                queue.append((exploring_x, exploring_y))
                maze[exploring_y][exploring_x] = 2

    return False
```

This solution makes use of the breadth-first search algorithm to find the path from start to end. It starts from the start position and explores all the possible paths to reach the end position. It keeps track of the visited positions and changes the value from 0 to 2 to avoid revisiting the same cell. If it reaches the end position it returns *True* else *False*.

Let's break down the solution further:

1. We initialise the *num_rows* and *num_cols* variables to store the number of rows and columns in the maze, respectively.

2. A *queue* is created to store the positions to be explored. The *start_pos* is added to the queue initially.

3. The maze is modified to mark the starting position as visited by setting *maze[start_pos[1]][start_pos[0]]* to 2.

4. The main loop starts, which continues until the queue becomes empty, inside the loop:

    a. The current position is obtained by dequeuing from the front of the queue using *queue.pop(0)*. The *curr_x* and *curr_y* variables store the coordinates of the current position.

    b. If the current position is the same as the *end_pos*, it means the target has been reached and the function returns *True*.

    c. Otherwise, the code explores the adjacent positions to the current position in the order of right, left, down and up. The coordinates of these positions are stored in the *exploring_x* and *exploring_y* variables.

    d. For each adjacent position, the code checks if it is within the boundaries of the maze (0 <= *exploring_x* < *num_rows* and 0 <= *exploring_y* < *num_cols*) and if it is a valid path (*maze[exploring_y][exploring_x]* == 0).

        i. If the adjacent position is valid, it is added to the queue for further exploration, and the maze is marked as visited by setting *maze[exploring_y][exploring_x]* to 2.

5. If the loop completes without finding the target, it means there is no valid path from the starting position to the target, and the function returns *False*.

In summary, this code uses a BFS algorithm to explore the maze starting from the given *start_pos*. It checks adjacent positions and marks them as visited while using a queue to keep track of the positions to explore. If the target position *end_pos* is reached, the function returns *True*; otherwise, it returns *False* indicating no valid path exists.

Puzzle 48

```python
from __future__ import annotations
from typing import Iterator

def traverse_inorder(root_node: TreeNode | None)
    -> Iterator[int]:

    if root_node is None:
        return []

    yield from traverse_inorder(root_node.left)
    yield root_node.val
    yield from traverse_inorder(root_node.right)
```

In our solution here we make use of recursion to traverse the binary tree in in-order traversal order. It works as follows:

1. Firstly, we define a base case: `if root_node is None` - it means the tree is empty, so an empty list is returned.

2. If the *root_node* is not *None*, the code continues with the recursive traversal:

   a. The code first recursively traverses the left subtree by calling *traverse_inorder(root_node.left)*. The *yield from* keyword is used to yield each value returned by the recursive call to *traverse_inorder(root_node.left)*.

   b. After yielding all the values of the left subtree, the code yields the value of the current node (*yield root_node.val*).

   c. Finally, the code recursively traverses the right subtree by calling *traverse_inorder(root_node.right)*. Again, the *yield from* keyword is used to yield each value returned by the recursive call to *traverse_inorder(root_node.right)*.

The recursion continues until it reaches the leaves of the tree (when *root_node* becomes *None*), and then it backtracks, yielding values in the correct order based on the inorder traversal.

Puzzle 48.1 - Bonus Solution

```python
from __future__ import annotations
from typing import Iterator

def morris_traverse_inorder(root_node: TreeNode | None)
    -> Iterator[int]:

    current_node = root_node

    while current_node is not None:

        if current_node.left is None:
            yield current_node.val
            current_node = current_node.right

        else:
            predecessor_node = current_node.left

            while predecessor_node.right is not None
                and predecessor_node.right is not current_node:

                predecessor_node = predecessor_node.right

            if predecessor_node.right is None:
                predecessor_node.right = current_node
                current_node = current_node.left
            else:
                predecessor_node.right = None
                yield current_node.val
                current_node = current_node.right
```

This solution takes a *root_node* representing the root of the binary tree
and returns an iterator that yields the values of the nodes in the tree in
inorder traversal order.

1. We start by initialising the *current_node* variable with the
    root_node.

2. The code enters a loop that continues as long as *current_node* is
    not *None*.

3. Inside the loop, the code checks if the *current_node* has a left child.

    a. If it doesn't have a left child, it means it's the leftmost node in the current subtree, so the code yields its value and moves to the right child of the current node (*current_node = current_node.right*).

    b. Else, the code sets the predecessor node equal to the left child of the current node. It then checks if the predecessor has a right child and if that right child is not the *current_node*. This condition checks if the predecessor has already been visited in a previous traversal. The loop continues until it finds the predecessor or reaches the end of the right subtree of the predecessor.

        i. If the predecessor doesn't have a right child, it means it hasn't been visited yet. The code sets the right child of the predecessor to the *current_node* to establish the thread connecting them (*predecessor_node.right = current_node*). This thread allows the code to return to the current node after completing the in-order traversal of the predecessor's subtree. Then, the code moves to the left child of the *current_node* (*current_node = current_node.left*) to continue traversing the left subtree.

        ii. If the predecessor already has a right child (it has been visited in a previous traversal), the code removes the thread by setting the right child of the predecessor to *None* (*predecessor_node.right = None*). The code yields the value of the *current_node* since it has completed the inorder traversal of its left subtree. Finally, the code moves to the right child of the *current_node* (*current_node = current_node.right*) to traverse the right subtree.

4. The loop continues until all nodes in the binary tree have been visited and yielded.

Puzzle 49

```python
def solve_climbing_stairs_problem(total_stairs: int) -> int:
    if total_stairs == 0:
        return 0
    if total_stairs == 1:
        return 1
    if total_stairs == 2:
        return 2

    num_combinations = [0] * (total_stairs + 1)
    num_combinations[0] = 0
    num_combinations[1] = 1
    num_combinations[2] = 2

    for num_stairs in range(3, total_stairs + 1):
        num_combinations[num_stairs] = (
            num_combinations[num_stairs - 1]
                + num_combinations[num_stairs - 2]
        )
    return num_combinations[-1]
```

The code checks the base cases where the *total_stairs* are 0, 1, or 2. If *total_stairs* is 0, it means there are no stairs, so the function returns 0. If *total_stairs* is 1, there is only one way to climb the stairs (by taking a single step), so the function returns 1. If *total_stairs* is 2, there are two ways to climb the stairs (either by taking two steps at once or taking one step twice), so the function returns 2.

If the *total_stairs* is greater than 2, the code initialises a list called *num_combinations* with *total_stairs + 1* elements, all initially set to 0. This list will store the number of combinations for each number of stairs.

- The code assigns initial values to *num_combinations[0], [1]* and *[2]* as 0, 1 and 2 respectively. These values correspond to the base cases where *total_stairs* is 0, 1 or 2.

The code then uses a loop to calculate the number of combinations for each number of stairs from 3 to *total_stairs* + *1*. It iterates over the range and calculates the number of combinations for the current number of stairs by adding the previous two values from *num_combinations*.

Finally, the function returns the last element of the *num_combinations* list, which represents the total number of distinct ways to reach the top of the staircase with *total_stairs* steps.

The code utilises the concept of dynamic programming by storing and reusing previously calculated values to avoid redundant calculations. This approach improves the efficiency of solving the climbing stairs problem by avoiding repetitive computations.

Puzzle 49.1 - Bonus Solution

```
def solve_climbing_stairs_problem_with_output(
    total_stairs: int)
-> list[list[int]]:

    if total_stairs == 0:
        return []
    if total_stairs == 1:
        return [[1]]
    if total_stairs == 2:
        return [[1, 1], [2]]

    num_combinations = [[] for _ in range(total_stairs + 1)]
    num_combinations[0] = []
    num_combinations[1] = [[1]]
    num_combinations[2] = [[1, 1], [2]]

    for num_stairs in range(3, total_stairs + 1):
        for seq in num_combinations[num_stairs - 1]:
            num_combinations[num_stairs].append(seq + [1])
        for seq in num_combinations[num_stairs - 2]:
            num_combinations[num_stairs].append(seq + [2])

    return num_combinations[-1]
```

This solution uses a similar approach as before, but instead of using a single list to store the number of ways to climb the stairs, it uses a list of lists, where each sublist represents a way to climb the stairs. The function initialises the first three elements of the list of lists as [], [[1]] and [[1,1], [2]], which are the only three ways to climb 0, 1 and 2 stairs respectively.

The function then uses nested loops to fill the rest of the list of lists, the outer loop iterates through the number of stairs and the inner loops iterate over the existing sequences in the previous step and append 1 or 2 to the sequence, creating new sequences of ways to climb the stairs. Finally, the function returns the last element of the list of lists, which is a list of all the possible ways to climb the stairs.

236

Note: this modified solution has a time complexity of $O(2\texttt{\^{}}n)$ and a space complexity of $O(n*2\texttt{\^{}}n)$ since it needs to save all the possible ways to climb the stairs, which grows exponentially as the number of stairs increases.

Puzzle 49.2 - Bonus Solution

```python
def solve_climbing_stairs_problem_with_three_steps_allowed(
    total_stairs: int
) -> int:

    if total_stairs == 0:
        return 0
    if total_stairs == 1:
        return 1
    if total_stairs == 2:
        return 2
    if total_stairs == 3:
        return 4

    num_combinations = [0] * (total_stairs + 1)
    num_combinations[0] = 0
    num_combinations[1] = 1
    num_combinations[2] = 2
    num_combinations[3] = 4

    for num_stairs in range(4, total_stairs + 1):
        num_combinations[num_stairs] = (
            num_combinations[num_stairs - 1]
            + num_combinations[num_stairs - 2]
            + num_combinations[num_stairs - 3]
        )
    return num_combinations[total_stairs]
```

You'll notice this solution is very similar to the original solution, all we have to do is make some small modifications to accommodate for one, two or three steps being taken. These modifications are:

1. A new base case where *total_stairs* equals 3, in this case we return 4 as there are four ways to go up the stairs ([1,1,1], [1,2], [2,1], [3]).

2. A new entry into the *num_combinations* list for index 3 = 4.

3. A new addition when calculating the next *num_combinations[num_stairs]* value (*num_combinations[num_stairs - 3]*).

Puzzle 50

```python
def solve_coin_change_problem(
    coin_values: list[int],
    target_amount: int
) -> int:

    if target_amount == 0:
        return 0

    if coin_values == []:
        return -1

    min_num_coins = [float("inf")] * (target_amount + 1)
    min_num_coins[0] = 0

    for current_target_amount in range(1, target_amount + 1):
        for current_coin_value in coin_values:

            if current_target_amount - current_coin_value >= 0:
                min_num_coins[current_target_amount] = min(
                    min_num_coins[current_target_amount],
                    min_num_coins[current_target_amount
                        - current_coin_value] + 1,
                )

    return int(min_num_coins[target_amount])
```

The code first checks two base cases:

1. If the *target_amount* is 0, it means we don't need any coins to reach the target amount, so the function returns 0.

2. If the *coin_values* list is empty, it means there are no coins available, so it's impossible to make up the target amount. In this case, the function returns -1 to indicate that it's not possible to make the change.

The code initialises a list called *min_num_coins* with *target_amount + 1* elements, all initially set to infinity (*float("inf")*). This list will store the minimum number of coins needed to make up each target amount from 0 to *target_amount*.

The code sets *min_num_coins[0]* to 0 since we don't need any coins to make up an amount of 0.

The code uses nested loops to calculate the minimum number of coins needed for each target amount from 1 to *target_amount*. The outer loop iterates over the range 1 to *target_amount + 1*, representing the current target amount. The inner loop iterates over the *coin_values* list and considers each coin value as a potential coin to be used.

1. Inside the inner loop, the code checks if subtracting the current coin value from the current target amount (*current_target_amount - current_coin_value*) results in a non-negative value. If it does, it means the current coin can contribute to the target amount.

2. The code updates *min_num_coins[current_target_amount]* by taking the minimum value between its current value and the sum of *min_num_coins[current_target_amount - current_coin_value] + 1*. This represents the minimum number of coins needed to make up the current target amount, considering the current coin.

After the loops complete, the function returns the integer value of *min_num_coins[target_amount]*, which represents the minimum number of coins needed to make up the target amount.

The code utilises the concept of dynamic programming by storing and reusing previously calculated values in the *min_num_coins* list. This approach allows the algorithm to avoid redundant calculations and find the optimal solution efficiently.

Fun Puzzles: Solutions

Reverse DNS Lookup

```python
import socket

def reverse_dns_lookup(ip_address: str) -> str:
    try:
        domain_name = socket.gethostbyaddr(ip_address)[0]
        return domain_name
    except socket.herror:
        return None
```

This solution performs a reverse DNS lookup using the *socket.gethostbyaddr()* function. This function takes an IP address as input and returns a tuple containing the domain name and additional information.

If the reverse DNS lookup is successful, the function retrieves the domain name from the returned tuple and returns it as a string.

However, if an exception of type socket.herror occurs during the reverse DNS lookup, it means that the lookup failed. In this case, the function handles the exception and returns *None* to indicate that no domain name was found for the given IP address.

To use this code, you need to import the socket module before calling the *reverse_dns_Lookup* function. The socket module provides networking functionality in Python, including the ability to perform DNS lookups.

Russian Dolls

```python
from __future__ import annotations

class RussianDoll:
    def __init__(
            self,
            size: int,
            colour: str,
            child_doll: RussianDoll | None = None
    ) -> None:

        self.size = size
        self.colour = colour
        self.child_doll = child_doll

    def get_number_of_children(self) -> int:
        if self.child_doll is None:
            return 0
        return 1 + self.child_doll.get_number_of_children()

    def print_unpack(self) -> None:
        print(
            f"Unpacking a {self.colour} doll of size: "
            f"{self.size} with {self.get_number_of_children()} "
            f"nested dolls inside."
        )

def unpack_dolls(doll: RussianDoll) -> int:
    print(f"Total number of dolls unpacked: "
            f"{inner_unpack_dolls(doll)}")


def inner_unpack_dolls(doll: RussianDoll) -> int:

    doll.print_unpack()

    if doll.child_doll is None:
        return 1

    return 1 + inner_unpack_dolls(doll.child_doll)
```

This solution makes use of three additional functions to what was originally given in the starter code:

It starts with *inner_unpack_dolls* - this function does a few different things:

1. Unpacks the current doll by calling the dolls *print_unpack* method. This outputs the "Unpacking a {self.colour} doll of size: {self.size} with {self.get_number_of_children()} nested dolls inside" line to the console.

    a. This makes use of the dolls *get_number_of_children* method. This method makes use of recursion to work out how many child dolls the doll has inside of it.

2. Checks if the doll has a child inside of it, if it doesn't then 1 is returned (this is the base case for recursion).

3. Calls the recursive step to unpack the dolls inside of the current doll. This not only unpacks the rest of the dolls but also keeps a count of how many total dolls have been unpacked. This value is then returned back to the *unpack_dolls* function.

Fractal Tree

```python
import turtle

def draw_tree(depth: int) -> None:
    if depth == 0:
        return
    turtle.forward(20*depth)
    turtle.left(30)
    draw_tree(depth-1)
    turtle.right(60)
    draw_tree(depth-1)
    turtle.left(30)
    turtle.backward(20*depth)

draw_tree(5)
turtle.exitonclick()
```

The provided code uses the turtle module in Python to draw a tree-like pattern on a graphics window. Here's a step-by-step explanation of how it works:

1. We define a base case that checks if depth is equal to 0.

   a. If the base case is hit, it means that the recursion has reached the desired depth, and the function simply returns, effectively stopping further recursion.

2. If the base case is not met, the function continues to execute. The turtle moves forward by a distance of 20 * *depth* units. The depth parameter is used to control the length of each branch based on the depth level.

3. The turtle then turns left by 30 degrees to change its direction.

4. The *draw_tree* function is called recursively, each time with a reduced depth value (*depth-1*). This creates a branching effect as the tree expands. The recursion is responsible for drawing the sub-trees on the left and right sides of the current branch.

5. After the recursive calls, the turtle turns right by 60 degrees to prepare for drawing the next branch.

6. Another recursive call to *draw_tree* is made with the reduced depth value to draw the next branch in the opposite direction.

7. The turtle turns left by 30 degrees to restore its original orientation.

8. Finally, the turtle moves backward by the same distance it moved forward earlier (20 * *depth* units), effectively returning to the starting position of the current branch.

The *turtle.exitonclick()* function is called to keep the turtle graphics window open until the user clicks on it to close.

Ping Pong

This solution is too big to print directly in the book, so can be found over on the github repository. Here is a short link to it: https://rb.gy/6n2rq

Once you have the solution open, here is how it works:

1. The code starts by importing the necessary modules: *pygame* for game development and *sys* for system-specific parameters and functions. The pygame library is initialised by calling *pygame.init()*.

2. Several constants are defined, including the width and height of the game window, the frames per second, paddle dimensions, paddle movement speed, and various thresholds and sizes related to the ball and scoring.

3. Variables are set to store the initial positions of the paddles, the ball, and the scores.

4. A game window is created using *pygame.display.set_mode()* with the specified width and height. The window's title is set using *pygame.display.set_caption()*.

5. Two paddle objects (*left_paddle* and *right_paddle*) are created as *pygame.Rect* objects. These rectangles represent the paddles' positions and dimensions.

6. The main game loop is created, which continues indefinitely until the game is exited. Inside the loop:

    a. Events are handled using *pygame.event.get()*. If the *pygame.QUIT* event is triggered (e.g., the user closes the game window), the game is terminated by calling *pygame.quit()* and *sys.exit()*.

    b. The code checks for user input to move the paddles. It uses *pygame.key.get_pressed()* to check if certain keys (e.g., W, S, UP, DOWN) are being pressed. Based on the input, the position of the paddles is updated, considering the defined thresholds for the top and bottom of the screen.

c. The ball's position is updated by adding the *ball_speed* vector to the current position.

d. Collision detection is performed to check if the ball collides with either paddle. The code checks if the ball's x-coordinate is in line with a paddle, and if the ball's y-coordinate is within the paddle's vertical range. If a collision occurs, and the ball is moving towards the paddle, the ball's x-speed is reversed.

e. The code checks if the ball hits the top or bottom of the screen, and if so, reverses the y-speed to bounce the ball back into play.

f. Point scoring is checked by comparing the ball's x-coordinate with the scoring thresholds. If the ball goes past the left scoring threshold, the right player scores a point, and the ball is reset to its starting position. If the ball goes past the right scoring threshold, the left player scores a point, and the ball is reset.

g. The game screen is filled with a black colour using *screen.fill()*. Then, the paddles and the ball are drawn on the screen using *pygame.draw.rect()* and *pygame.draw.circle()*, respectively.

h. The current score is rendered as a text using the specified font and size with the help of *FONT.render()*. The rendered text is then displayed on the screen using *screen.blit()*.

i. The game display is updated using *pygame.display.update()*, and the frame rate is controlled using *clock.tick(FPS)*, ensuring the game runs at the specified frames per second. The loop continues, and the game state is updated in subsequent iterations.

Ping Pong - Bonus

This solution is too big to print directly in the book, so can be found over on the github repository. Here is a short link to it: https://rb.gy/p951y

This solution introduces some additional features compared to the previous code. Here's how it works:

1. The code starts by importing the necessary modules: *pygame*, *sys*, *math*, and *random*. The *pygame.init()* function is called to initialise the pygame library.

2. The code defines two classes: *StaticColour* and *ChangingColour*. These classes represent different types of colours that can be used in the game. *StaticColour* stores a fixed colour value, while *ChangingColour* can cycle through a list of colours. The *ChangingColour* class uses the *pygame.time.set_timer()* function to trigger a custom event (*pygame.USEREVENT*) every 500 milliseconds, which is used to change the colour periodically.

3. The *ColourPicker* class is defined to facilitate colour selection in the game. It includes various predefined colours and allows the player to pick a colour for different game elements, such as the background, paddles, and ball. The *select_colour()* method is the main entry point for colour selection. It displays a window where the player can choose from available colours by clicking on colour squares. The selected colour is returned by the method.

4. The *Ball* class represents a ball in the game. It has attributes for position, speed, size, and colour. The class provides methods for moving the ball, resetting its position, and changing its direction. The *get_colour()* method returns the current colour of the ball.

5. The *Paddle* class represents a paddle in the game. It has attributes for position, dimensions, speed, and colour. The class provides methods for moving the paddle up and down, retrieving the colour, and converting the paddle to a *pygame.Rect* object.

6. The *PingPong* class encapsulates the game logic and serves as the main entry point. It defines various constants for screen size, paddle and ball properties, and game settings.

7. In the *PingPong* constructor, the game window is created using *pygame.display.set_mode()*, and the window's title is set. The player is prompted to choose colours for the background, paddles, and ball using the *ColourPicker* class.

8. The *create_balls()* method initialises the balls for the game. It creates multiple instances of the *Ball* class with random starting speeds and positions.

9. The *play()* method is the main game loop. It continuously handles events, updates the game state, and renders the screen:

   a. The *handle_event()* method handles different events, such as quitting the game, mouse button presses for colour selection, and the custom *pygame.USEREVENT* for periodic colour changing. It updates the colours of game objects if they are of type *ChangingColour*.

   b. The *handle_paddle_movement()* method handles paddle movement based on user input. It checks for key presses and moves the paddles accordingly.

   c. The *ball_is_hit_by_paddle()* method checks if a ball collides with either paddle. It performs collision detection based on the positions and sizes of the paddles and the ball.

   d. The *ball_touched_top_or_bottom_of_screen()* method checks if a ball hits the top or bottom of the screen, requiring a change in its vertical direction.

   e. The *left_scoring_threshold_hit()* and *right_scoring_threshold_hit()* methods check if a ball crosses the scoring thresholds on the left or right side of the screen, indicating a point scored by the opposing player.

   f. The *draw()* method handles the drawing of game objects on the screen. It fills the screen with the background colour, draws the paddles and balls, and displays the current score.

Finally, the *PingPong()* class is instantiated, and the *play()* method is called to start the game.

Drawing Tool

```python
import pygame
import sys


pygame.init()


class DrawingTool:

    SCREEN_WIDTH, SCREEN_HEIGHT = 800, 600
    PAINT_SIZE = 10

    def __init__(self):

        # Create a window
        self.screen = pygame.display.set_mode(
            (DrawingTool.SCREEN_WIDTH,
             DrawingTool.SCREEN_HEIGHT))
        pygame.display.set_caption("Drawing Tool")

        self.is_drawing = False

    def start(self):
        while True:
            for event in pygame.event.get():
                if event.type == pygame.QUIT:
                    pygame.quit()
                    sys.exit()
                if event.type == pygame.MOUSEBUTTONDOWN:
                    self.is_drawing = True
                if event.type == pygame.MOUSEBUTTONUP:
                    self.is_drawing = False

            if self.is_drawing:
                self.draw(pygame.mouse.get_pos())

            pygame.display.update()
```

```
def draw(self, pos):
        pygame.draw.circle(
                self.screen,
                (255, 255, 255),
                pos,
                DrawingTool.PAINT_SIZE
        )

if __name__ == "__main__":
    DrawingTool().start()
```

Let's go through the solution step by step to understand how it works:

1. The code starts by importing the necessary modules: *pygame* for game development and *sys* for system-specific parameters and functions. The pygame library is initialised by calling *pygame.init()*.

2. A class called *DrawingTool* is defined to encapsulate the functionality of the drawing tool. The *DrawingTool* class has several class-level constants defined:

    a. *SCREEN_WIDTH* and *SCREEN_HEIGHT* represent the dimensions of the drawing window.

    b. *PAINT_SIZE* represents the size of the brush used for drawing.

3. The *__init__* method of *DrawingTool* initialises the drawing window and sets the window caption. It also initialises the *is_drawing* variable to *False*, indicating that the user is not currently drawing.

5. The start method is the main loop of the program. It continuously runs until the program is exited. Inside the loop, it handles any events raised by the user (such as mouse clicks or window close events).

   a. If the user clicks the close button on the window, *pygame.quit()* is called to quit pygame, and *sys.exit()* is called to exit the program.

   b. If the user presses the mouse button down, *self.is_drawing* is set to *True*, indicating that the user has started drawing. If the user releases the mouse button, *self.is_drawing* is set to *False*, indicating that the user has stopped drawing. Additionally, if the *is_drawing* flag is *True*, it calls the draw method and passes the current mouse position obtained using *pygame.mouse.get_pos()*.

6. The *draw* method takes the position argument and uses the *pygame.draw.circle* function to draw a white circle on the screen at the given position with a radius equal to *DrawingTool.PAINT_SIZE*. This creates the effect of drawing on the screen.

Finally, *DrawingTool().start()* is used to start execution of the program.

Drawing Tool - Bonus

This solution is too big to print directly in the book, so can be found over on the github repository. Here is a short link to it: https://rb.gy/tp9qe

Let's go through the code step by step to understand how it works:

1. The code begins by importing the *pygame*, *sys*, and *product* modules. Pygame for game development, sys for system-specific parameters and functions, and product is used to generate cartesian products. The pygame library is initialised by calling *pygame.init()*.

2. The *DrawingTools* class is defined with two class-level variables: *PAINT_BRUSH* and *LINE_TOOL*. These variables represent different drawing tools available in the program.

3. The *ActionButtons* class is defined with four class-level variables: *CLEAR_CANVAS*, *SAVE_IMAGE*, *PLUS_THICKNESS*, and *MINUS_THICKNESS*. These variables represent different action buttons available in the program.

4. The *DrawingTool* class is defined to encapsulate the functionality of the drawing tool. It has several constants defined:

    a. *SCREEN_WIDTH* and *SCREEN_HEIGHT* represent the dimensions of the drawing window.

    b. *SIDEBAR_COLOUR* represents the colour of the sidebar in the drawing window.

    c. *SIDEBAR_BUTTON_COLOUR* represents the colour of the buttons in the sidebar.

    d. *SIDEBAR_WIDTH* represents the width of the sidebar.

    e. *SIDEBAR_NUM_COLS* represents the number of columns in the sidebar.

    f. *SIDEBAR_BUTTONS_RECT_SIZE* represents the size of the buttons in the sidebar.

g. *THICKNESS_INCREMEMT* represents the increment value for changing the drawing thickness.

h. *BACKGROUND_COLOUR* represents the background colour of the drawing canvas.

i. *BACKGROUND_Y* and *BACKGROUND_X* represent the starting position of the drawing canvas.

5. The constructor of the *DrawingTool* class initialises the drawing window and sets the window caption. It also initialises various variables such as *is_drawing* (indicating if the user is currently drawing), *is_draw_line_mode* (indicating if the line drawing mode is enabled), *line_initial_point* (the initial point for drawing a line), *drawing_colour* (the colour used for drawing), *drawing_tool* (the current drawing tool selected), *drawing_snapshot* (a snapshot of the drawing canvas), and *thickness* (the current drawing thickness).

6. The start method is the main loop of the program. It first calls the *clear_canvas* method to clear the drawing canvas. Inside the loop, it handles any events raised by the user (such as mouse clicks or window close events).

a. If the user clicks the close button on the window, *pygame.quit()* is called to quit *pygame*, and *sys.exit()* is called to exit the program.

b. If the user presses the mouse button down, the *handle_mouse_button_down* method is called.

c. If the user releases the mouse button, the *handle_mouse_button_up* method is called.

7. The *render_side_bar* method is responsible for rendering the sidebar of the drawing tool. It creates a dictionary called *clickables* to store clickable rectangles. It renders the background of the sidebar, renders the colour options, renders the action buttons, and renders the thickness selector. It returns the clickables dictionary.

8. The *render_sidebar_colour_options* method renders the colour options in the sidebar. It uses the *product* function from the *itertools* module to generate all possible combinations of RGB values (0 and 255). It then iterates over the colours and renders rectangles for each colour option. It adds the rectangles to the clickables dictionary.

9. The *render_sidebar_action_buttons* method renders the action buttons in the sidebar. It uses a list of predefined tools and buttons and iterates over them to render rectangles and text for each button. It adds the rectangles to the *clickables* dictionary.

10. The *render_thickness_selector* method renders the thickness selector in the sidebar. It renders the minus and plus buttons for decreasing and increasing the thickness, respectively. It also renders the current thickness value. It adds the buttons to the *clickables* dictionary.

11. The *handle_mouse_button_down* method is called when the mouse button is pressed down. If the background of the drawing canvas is clicked, it checks the current drawing tool. If the tool is a paintbrush, *is_drawing* is set to *True*, indicating that the user is currently drawing. If the tool is a line tool, *is_draw_line_mode* is toggled, and if it becomes *True*, it takes a snapshot of the current drawing canvas and saves the initial mouse position for drawing a line.

12. The *handle_mouse_button_up* method is called when the mouse button is released. If the background of the drawing canvas is clicked, it checks the current drawing tool. If the tool is a paintbrush, *is_drawing* is set to *False*, indicating that the user has stopped drawing. If the mouse is not clicked on the drawing canvas, it calls the *action_sidebar_btn_pressed* method.

13. The *action_sidebar_btn_pressed* method is called when an action button or a colour option is pressed in the sidebar. It checks which colour option or button is clicked and performs the corresponding action. For colour options, it updates the current drawing colour. For action buttons, it updates the current drawing tool, clears the canvas, saves the image, or modifies the thickness value.

14. The *clear_canvas* method clears the drawing canvas by drawing a background rectangle with the specified background colour.

15. The *save_image* method saves the current drawing as an image. It creates a subsurface of the screen using the background rectangle as the area to be saved. If *save_to_disk* is *True*, it saves the subsurface as an image file. It returns the subsurface.

16. The draw method is responsible for drawing circles on the screen at the given position with the specified thickness and colour.

17. The *draw_line* method is responsible for drawing a line on the screen between the initial mouse position and the current mouse position. It also draws circles at the endpoints of the line to create a rounded line effect.

Finally, *DrawingTool().start()* is used to start execution of the program.

www.ingramcontent.com/pod-product-compliance
Lightning Source LLC
LaVergne TN
LVHW051443050326
832903LV00030BD/3212